FAMIL

HOW
THE
BEST MAN

Dedication
To the Best Man

FAMILY MATTERS

HOW TO BE THE THE BEST MAN

ANGELA LANSBURY

WARD LOCK

First published in Great Britain in 1989
by Ward Lock Limited, Villiers House,
41–47 Strand, London WC2N 5JE, a Cassell company.

Reprinted 1989, 1990, 1991

Illustrations by John Woodcock
Text filmset in Sabon
by MS Filmsetting Limited, Frome, Somerset
Printed and bound in Great Britain by
William Collins Sons & Co Ltd, Glasgow

British Library Cataloguing in Publication Data
Lansbury, Angela
How to be the best man.—(Family matters).
1. Weddings. Planning – For the best man
I. Title   II. Series
395'.22

ISBN 0-7063-6748-0

CONTENTS

Introduction · 6
Choosing the Best Man · 8
When You Are Chosen · 14
Organizing the Stag Party · 21
Pre-wedding Plans · 30
The Wedding Day · 37
Preparing the Best Man's Speech · 47
At the Reception · 51
Informal Weddings · 58
Duties for Different Ceremonies and
Customs · 60
After the Party · 74
After the Honeymoon · 77
Troubleshooting Guide · 81
Instant Checklist of Best Man's Duties · 93
Index · 95

INTRODUCTION

When a wedding is planned the bridegroom must choose a suitable best man, and decide upon the number of ushers and how much help to ask from them. The best man and ushers who wonder what they are required to do must be told. This depends on the size and style of the wedding. It is simple and great fun when you know how.

The duties of the best man can range considerably. The easiest job is that of the best man who merely signs the register on the happy occasion and gets dinner and free drinks as a reward. The most time-consuming role is that of the best man who has to organize a grand wedding where even people as important as foreign Heads of State are invited. The transport, church seating, and protocol of precedence involve such a complex battle strategy that if he had known all the details in advance he might have backed out in horror! Yet the more the best man has to arrange, the more rewarding his job is in the long run. Most weddings fall between these two extremes.

The ushers have less to do. But like all people involved in a wedding they are part of a team. The success of the day depends on co-ordinating with others in advance and their reliable and good-humoured behaviour at the appointed time.

When you watch someone else's wedding it usually looks effortlessly done. Only when you are involved in a wedding do you suddenly realize that you are faced with questions about whether to stand on the left or right, what to say, and who to toast and thank in a speech. The sample speeches, and variations for different ceremonies should help you on the happy occasion, make interesting reading, and suggest new ideas to you.

Some people view the approach of a wedding with

unnecessary fears about getting it right, and overcoming potential problems. Careful planning, using the checklist at the end of the book, will cover most eventualities. Yet it is a mistake to be over-confident. On a recent radio programme listeners phoned in with funny stories about narrowly averted wedding disasters. One best man escorted the groom to the wrong church. Another best man stood in the groom's place by mistake, prompted the tongue-tied groom in stage whispers, and discovered the minister had married the bride to the best man. None of this will happen to you of course, because you will have read the troubleshooting guide, and will be determined to be much more careful.

This book will help you prepare so that everything goes smoothly on the important day which means so much to you, your family and friends. Acting as best man or usher should be the satisfying culmination of your friendship with the groom, and the start or continuation of a lifelong friendship with him and his bride. You should be pleased and proud, with many happy memories.

CHOOSING THE BEST MAN

This chapter is intended as guidance for the groom and bridal couple, but it will be of interest to the best man.

INFLUENCE FROM OLDEN TIMES

Legacies of real or imaginary tales of grooms abducting brides with the assistance of their best man can be seen in the ritual of the modern church wedding. The groom has his right hand free to ward off attackers and the bride stands on his left. The groom wears a sword on his left ready to be drawn out and brandished on the right. (It is said that Prince Charles sensibly wanted to change this tradition because the sword might have damaged Diana's dress.) The best man stands near the groom in order to defend him. Later he acts as witness by signing the register.

Why Brothers are Favoured

Until about one hundred years ago families were larger than those of today so it would have been usual for the best man to be a brother of the groom. Similarly the bride's chief bridesmaid or matron of honour would have been her oldest sister or the sister closest in age. Nowadays with fewer brothers and sisters available it is common to choose a close cousin. Traditionally the first choice would have been a brother, the second choice a cousin, the third choice a friend. To have elevated a friend above a brother might have implied some shortcoming on the part of the brother and caused ill-feeling within the family.

Why Relatives are Preferred

The close relationship of the groom and best man is important. The best man is selected from all the available relatives and friends. He will probably be invited to subsequent family reunions, making a member of the family a good choice. He appears on wedding photographs which remain for many years. So you will have to choose somebody you like and expect to remain in touch with during the years ahead. This matters even if you ask him to do no more than turn up on the day carrying the ring.

The Role of the Best Man Today

The duties of the best man nowadays are mainly administrative, combined with moral support. If practical help is urgently needed, for example by a groom who is away in the armed services, he must choose a person he can rely upon to organize matters in his absence. However when several members of the family can help, the groom can adapt the duties imposed on the best man. A shy, introverted, conscientious younger brother might be best man in charge of the lists, and ring, but spared the responsibility of making a speech. The extrovert, confident older married brother who treats life as a joke and is so easy-going you fear he might lose the ring, could give the wedding toast and a speech guaranteed to make everyone laugh.

THE GROOM'S CHOICE

The best man is the groom's chief assistant and companion during the wedding and the groom decides who should be best man. Naturally the groom will consult the family and the potential candidate, or candidates, before announcing his decision.

The groom and potential best man must consider the timing and costs involved. A married brother living overseas would have to decide whether to finance himself alone, possibly leaving behind a pregnant wife, or pay for the wife and children to come along – quite an expense. The wedding date may have to be moved so the best man can attend, or the groom may have to change his choice of best man.

How Soon to Decide

When the wedding is imminent the best man is chosen as soon as possible so he can assist with arrangements. Long engagements are rare these days, though, if the couple plan to marry when their studies end, it is better to delay choosing the best man. This especially applies when a friend is chosen because friendships change when companions take jobs some distance away or even abroad.

Financial Factors

A large wedding can impose many duties, of both cost and time, on a young man. The family may feel that a student younger brother, for example, should be concentrating on his studies, especially if his final exams are near the date of the wedding.

The best man may have to fund inter-city travel, or travelling back to Britain for the wedding, or an expensive trip to the bride's family home abroad. Accommodation, food, wedding clothes, the wedding present, and unforeseen expenses may strain the budget. The friend chosen because he made a good speech at another mutual friend's recent wedding has already had to find all these expenses once, yet he may have bought the required clothes, and wedding gifts by the dozen, and have his speech half prepared.

Subsidizing the Best Man's Travel

The family might pool transport by car or subsidize the travel expenses of the impecunious brother. An impecunious friend who is too proud to accept the offer, but is travelling with a large group of guests could possibly obtain discounts with a party booking. Hotels and travel companies or package tour operators may offer a free place to the organizer of a large group.

The person who declines to be best man is still invited to the wedding, which will involve the same travel expenses on the day. He is likely to send a gift even if he cannot afford the time and money to attend. The groom might like to suggest to a younger brother that what would be most appreciated would be a DIY gift such as a bookshelf, which would not involve great expense. If the brother or friend declines to be best man, or if there are two competing claims, one can be appointed as best man, the other as head usher.

USHERS

Do you need ushers? A bride with no brothers and sisters, or one entering a second marriage, might have a wedding with a best man but no bridesmaids or ushers. A small wedding at a register office, chapel or church does not require ushers.

The Number of Ushers

Ushers are needed at a formal wedding in a church or other religious building to show guests to their seats and to hand out order of service sheets. A general rule is one usher for every fifty guests.

Ushers' Expenses

Ushers, like the best man, will be involved in the expenses of travel, accommodation, clothes and a wedding gift. Although the groom is not expected to pay for their accommodation, he can save them the expense of staying in a hotel by installing out-of-town ushers at the homes of relatives.

Ushers pay for their own suits. The groom pays only for their matching ties, gloves and buttonholes (carnations or whatever).

Eligible Ushers

Are the bride's family eligible for the roles of ushers? Normally the groom has enough brothers or friends to be ushers. But just as the bride would be sensible to honour the groom's sister by appointing her as a bridesmaid, the groom would want to appoint the bride's brother as an usher, preferably chief usher. The usual rules of precedence apply, with the groom's brothers first, then the bride's, then friends. If the groom's first brother is best man and his second brother is chief usher, the bride's brother could be another usher.

UNUSUAL CHOICES OF BEST MAN

Bridegroom's Father

It is unusual to choose the bridegroom's father as best man because the groom usually has a brother, cousin or young friend of his own age to fill the role. The father is usually content to accompany his wife and the groom's parents in the Recession. The bride's father has a larger role and gives a speech, but then he is normally paying for the party and acting as host. But the groom might choose to give prominence to his own father in the event of war, travel overseas, and if the father is paying for part or all of the wedding. It might also be a way of including a father who wishes to have a particular role, or a generous way of including a stepfather, widower, or a father who cannot be with his wife – for instance, if she is in hospital – during the ceremony.

Best Girl

A rare modern innovation is the best girl – a female organizer, attendant, supporter, and companion for the groom. While this may appeal on the grounds of feminism and equal opportunity, it does leave the groom surrounded by large numbers of ladies. When there is a best girl the proportion of the sexes can be maintained and balanced by a male usher or two.

Being best girl can give a prominent role to an important extra lady, for example if the groom has a twin sister but the bride has already selected her own sister as chief bridesmaid. Or a groom travelling to the bride's home in a foreign country might not have a suitable close male companion.

THE IDEAL BEST MAN

The worst man for best man is one likely to hinder the groom, the wedding procedure, and the relationship of bride and groom, instead of helping. The best man should be chief executive but not want to be the groom's boss, nor the groom's rival for the bride – nor a practical joker!

It is more convenient if the best man lives nearby, not abroad. He should have a reliable chararacter, inspiring and showing evidence of being trustworthy, reliable, punctual, and discreet. The ideal best man combines the good attributes of a teacher, consultant, confessor, psychologist, manager, executive director, security guard, bodyguard, orator, diplomat when dealing with bride and in-laws, godfather, and marriage guidance counsellor.

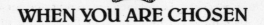

WHEN YOU ARE CHOSEN

You may be chosen as best man, anticipating the delightful prospect of dressing up at a grand wedding and making a speech. To be chosen as best man is an honour. You are a close relative or friend of the groom, and he is relying on you for assistance on one of the happiest and most important occasions in his life.

ACCEPTING THE ROLE OF BEST MAN

Are you going to accept? Why not? Should you, must you, can you? First check the wedding dates. Assuming that you are not obliged to take a pre-arranged holiday abroad, go into hospital, or take an exam on the groom's intended wedding date, you should be able to express your desire to accept.

You may wish to consider the location of the wedding – if the bride lives far away for example, what expense and time the travelling will involve. Going to India can involve more than 24 hours flying, and you can hardly arrive just a few hours in advance, because of the risk of flight delays.

It is not usual for the groom to pay for the travel and accommodation expenses of the best man and ushers. If he paid the travel of ten people to India he would have to spend a considerable sum. But as a close relative or friend you may be able to stay with your family, or share travel expenses and hotel costs with another of the ushers or guests.

TACTFUL REFUSAL

To refuse is rather delicate. Sometimes a blunt expression of the problem and your regret is the best solution, by phone for speed. If you are going to be abroad, follow it up by a friendly letter along the lines of:

'It's just the week you are getting married. What bad luck! I'm really sorry I can't be there. But I hope you have a truly splendid day. I shall certainly be thinking of you and we all send our best wishes.'

A brother returning from abroad especially for the wedding would not have time to act as organizer in the months leading up to it. He can be given or ask for other roles instead, such as giving a speech, acting as toast-master, or being head usher.

In a second marriage the question arises of how much to involve the children from the first marriage. A widow re-marrying might wish to give a prominent role to a grown-up or teenage son. If the groom agreed, her son could be best man. Not every boy would feel at ease doing this. He, too, might prefer to be an usher.

If the groom wants you to be the best man when you can see that your older brother really expects to be chosen, as would be correct, you may be able to keep family peace by expressing a preference for being head usher. Pretend that you prefer less responsibility. The alternative is to suggest that your rival be appointed chief usher.

Find out from the groom what he thinks your re-sponsibilities will be. These depend on the circumstances of the wedding, the wedding size – which may increase as the period of the engagement lengthens – and the bridegroom's age, especially if he is a lot younger or older than you are.

WEDDING CLOTHES

It is up to the groom to tell you how formal the wedding will be. Clearly it would be absurd if you wore informal clothes when the rest of the bridal party was in formal clothing. If it is going to be a black tie or morning suit affair you do not have to buy a new outfit, but you will be responsible for its hire, together with providing a shirt, and your own shoes. The groom may advise you where to obtain them, or you could take on the task of comparing the different hire companies.

However, the groom may provide the ushers with matching ties and handkerchiefs and buttonholes to give the wedding group a unified look and enable them to be identified.

SPEECHES

As best man you are not always obliged to make a speech. It would be possible to have no speeches at the wedding. The groom may not require the best man's speech if there are no bridesmaids. Or he may simply have another older friend of the family, perhaps a colleague of the bride's father, proposing the toast to the couple, a reply from the groom, and then a reply from the bride's father.

BEST MAN'S WEDDING GIFT

Being invited to be best man gives you a closer relationship with the bridal couple, and the best man normally gives a larger wedding gift than he would have done had he been an ordinary guest.

As a close friend or relative, you will naturally want to give the happy couple a wedding present. It is usual for any guest to give a present after being invited to a wedding, whether you are able to attend or not, although the tendency is to give a larger present if you are attending. The best man, like close relatives, gives a larger present than more distant relatives and friends, although of course this depends upon his circumstances and budget.

BEST MAN'S WIFE OR GIRLFRIEND

Does being a best man give you more or less right to bring along your wife or girlfriend? Naturally your wife will be invited, though she will not be with you throughout the wedding.

While the fiancée or long-standing girlfriend would normally be invited, if you are changing girlfriends every other week, or likely to change girlfriends before the date of the wedding ceremony, the bride's mother will not necessarily want to send out invitations to a succession of your acquaintances. Nor will you necessarily want an ex-girlfriend to appear at the wedding as well as your new girlfriend when the time of the wedding comes around.

It is not right for a total stranger or very recent acquaintance to arrive at the wedding, just because you met her the week before and you hope she will become a long-term friend. Of course the size of the wedding affects this. You could not expect a new girlfriend to be invited at the last moment to a dinner where seating plans have already been made. But it is quite possible to ask if a girlfriend may come along to a stand-up buffet, providing the invitation comes from the bride's family (or host).

INVITATIONS

The printed invitations will probably be sent out about six weeks before the date of the wedding. The best man and ushers, as part of the wedding party, already know they will be present. Others must wait for their formal invitations. If your long-standing girlfriend lives at a distance, the groom's mother may ask you for your girlfriend's address in order to send her the invitation. If the bride's mother or wedding dinner host is more cautious she or he may decide to send an invitation to you 'and guest'.

If the invitation goes the best man and his wife, or the best man and his fiancée or girlfriend, he is responsible for a wedding gift from both of them. If a separate invitation is sent to the girlfriend, she may wish to send a separate gift, or contribute a proportion of the cost in order to enable you to buy a larger joint gift.

Ushers' Girlfriends

The single ushers – particularly if there are as many as six ushers, are less likely than the best man to be invited to bring along girlfriends who are unknown to the hosts.

The host may have printed only the number of invitations required for the guests, and not for the wedding party themselves. If you do not receive one but you know there are spares you can reasonably ask for one 'as a souvenir'.

The Groom's Older Brother

If you are married, you have had the experience of a wedding before. Therefore you are in a good position to help and advise, though you cannot expect your brother to do exactly as you did at your wedding.

Children

If the best man's wife or usher's wife is invited to the wedding it does not necessarily follow that their children will be invited to the reception. The children of the groom's or bride's brothers are probably known well to the bride and groom. If they are part of the ceremony as bridesmaids or page boys they will usually be invited to the reception, unless this is long past their usual bedtime in which case you must book a babysitter. (Remember that granny, other relatives, colleagues and neighbours may be busy at the wedding.)

When the bride has no bridesmaids and there is a seated dinner the wedding reception host may have good reasons for not including children. There is likely to be a limit to the number of seats, and to the cost of each dinner ordered from the caterers. Small children do not sit still easily during long dinners and speeches. If the bride's mother invites one set of children she may create ill-feeling if she does not invite the children of other brothers and cousins, which could add another thirty to the catering. Older teenagers are sometimes invited to come along if there is a dance after the seated dinner.

GROOM'S BEST FRIEND/WORKMATE, COLLEAGUE, OR BUSINESS PARTNER

If you do not already know the bride, the sooner you get to meet her and her family the better. When organizing the wedding, advising the groom, and writing your speech, you will want to appreciate the bride's family's lifestyle and fit in with her, as well as the groom's family's lifestyle and his aspirations. If your groom is of a different religion or nationality, check the location of the wedding, then what your responsibilities will be.

You are presumably chosen because the groom knows you well and likes you a great deal and has no brothers or close relatives. The bride's family will be regarding you as the groom's right hand man, representing his friends and the sort of person he is or would like to be, and your good conduct will reflect on him.

If you work with the groom, don't talk shop at the wedding in front of the family and the guests.

BEST GIRL

If you are not happy with the unconventional idea of being best girl, you might hint that you would be happier being maid or matron of honour, or chief bridesmaid. This might involve you in an equal amount of dressing up and fun, but with responsibility for helping the bride write invitations and thank you letters, dressing her, and organizing her clothes, rather than helping the groom with his clothes and the honeymoon – which is some-times supposed to be a secret from the bride.

Assuming that you accept, you will want to meet both sides of the family and make sure that they are happy with your role so that the ceremony goes as expected and having a best girl instead of a best man is not a big surprise to everyone.

At a formal wedding you will probably wear a smart day dress, perhaps with a corsage of fresh flowers pinned to your lapel bodice to distinguish you from the other guests. At a second marriage where the bride is wearing a suit, you could be similarly attired.

When the bride is not wearing white, the bride's mother and groom's mother are normally a generation older and can be distinguished from the younger bride. However, if you are of similar age to the bride and groom, or look young, you will want to ensure that the bride wears more distinctive clothes or flowers than you do. You should also avoid wearing an entire dress or large areas of colour which will clash with the rest of the wedding party. If the others are wearing pink and purple, that may rule out a bright orange or red dress and accessories.

Your clothes will be different from those of any bridesmaids, though if there are ushers you might have a corsage paid for by the groom, and a sash or shoes to echo the groom's family or team colour. If you are in the armed forces, you could also be co-ordinated with the groom and ushers by wearing a dress uniform of your military regiment.

Bridesmaids are required to wear dresses which are identical or co-ordinating with each other, often in a paler colour such as pink, or yellow and green, echoing the bride's dress and accessories. As best girl you also pay for your own outfit, but are not required to co-ordinate with the bride, matron of honour, or bridesmaids.

ORGANIZING THE STAG PARTY

A stag party is not obligatory but it is often staged by members of clubs and groups, particularly by all-male organizations such as football teams when one of their number is getting married. The best man is the organizer, but who is the host and who pays? The best man is the host and issues the invitations and therefore he pays, but usually with the help of those attending if it is a large gathering.

At a pub the best man would buy the first round of drinks. Probably others would then offer to pay for subsequent rounds, or at least for the groom's refills. At a restaurant dinner the best man organizes it, warning the guests in advance roughly what it will cost, having first verified this with the restaurant manager. At the end of the evening the bill is then split between the guests, with the exception of the groom who does not pay.

The guests will normally be mostly the groom's young friends – those he would go out with on a Saturday night, weekend nights, or see regularly for sports, rather than his elderly relatives. The guests can be the groom's choice or a surprise. It would be hard to stop well-wishers drifting along if you set off in a crowd from the office or held the event at your local pub. Numbers can range from the groom and best man having a drink together, to a small group such as the groom, best man and two ushers having dinner together, to a full scale party with 20 or more guests.

THE DATE OF THE STAG PARTY

A party which includes the groom and relatives or friends flying in from abroad specially for the wedding has to be held as near the wedding date as possible, but not the night before. The groom, best man and guests may have last minute arrangements to make for the wedding next day, and they want to be wide awake to enjoy the day, rather than dozing and hung over.

LOCATIONS

Possible locations are pubs, clubs, wine bars, restaurants, or private homes. If the stag party will be attended mainly by people from the workplace or office, the ideal location is a pub or other location near by. Many pubs have a separate room which can be hired or sometimes used at no cost.

The cheapest drinks party is one organized at somebody's home, with drinks bought in bulk, glasses borrowed from an off-licence, or paper cups used. If the home is that of the bridegroom or a best man who lives nearby, anyone who gets tipsy can stay there until they sober up enough to walk or drive home safely. You could start at the local and end up at home.

Food First

The first thing to provide at a party is food, otherwise guests will sneak off early to get something to eat. Sufficient food must be provided, something for later arrivals, and provision for those on a diet. Peanuts, prawns, pork sausages, sherry, beer, whisky, and spirits will leave most of your Jewish, Muslim and Hindu friends or workmates with little to eat and drink except peanuts and water. Orthodox Jews eat kosher meat and no shellfish. Muslims eat Halal meat. Hindus are vegetarian. Jews, Muslims and Hindus don't like to get drunk, so even if they are non-orthodox and imbibe, some of them will prefer low alcohol drinks rather than spirits. So try to include some cheese, vegetables, fruit, and wine. You must also have some juices, soft drinks, and non-alcoholic beers for the drivers.

Drinks and Jinks

Drinking on an empty stomach would make half of your

guests sleepy and the other half noisy and belligerent. You probably know the way your group behaves under the influence of drink. You must make sure that the guests have fun but matters do not get out of hand. It is the best man's job to ensure that no one gets too drunk, particularly the groom.

Sobering Up

Now it is generally known that drinking an excessive amount is dangerous and could have fatal consequences, even if the groom does not mix alcohol with drugs, or try to walk or drive home. There have been cases of grooms being delivered home unconscious and having to be hospitalized after drunken stag nights, which have never been popular with their brides. So you need to keep all the party reasonably sober, particularly the groom, or at least get them sobered up before they leave the premises.

Give the guests food before they start drinking, plus a liberal supply of non-alcoholic drinks. Mix a punch containing decreasing amounts of alcohol as you replenish it. Offer more food and coffee before they leave. Arrange entertainment to keep them busy and otherwise amused. If all else fails you will have to water down their subsequent drinks, 'lose' their car keys, and drive them home yourself or call a taxi.

ENTERTAINMENT

Rather than making the groom a source of unintended merriment, some form of entertainment can be organized. This can follow the interests of the groom himself or the group as a whole.

Be a Sport

If the groom is a keen sports player, arrange for him to have a professional coaching lesson to improve his play. Leisure centres hire sports facilities with a coach in attendance. You could snorkel in a swimming pool, have a deep sea diving lesson with a club, and take pictures with an underwater camera.

An afternoon could be spent watching or trying stock car racing, or spend an evening at the cinema. Or even spend a whole day on an organized Survival Game or some activity the groom's wife-to-be might not enjoy.

Photograph it, film it

Don't forget to take a photo of the groom in action. Both Polaroid and 35 mm cameras would be useful. Polaroid will provide instant pictures to pass around and discuss.

A conventional camera will take good quality photographs to be enlarged as souvenirs. The latest automatic 35 mm cameras made by Pentax have a zoom for close-ups. If the groom looks impressive perhaps a good photo can be blown up to poster size. The Polaroid photos of the stag party can also make an interesting beginning or end to wedding day photo albums.

Better still, record the groom's play on video: you can either hire a video camera for the day or get a company to take the video film for you. You might be able to arrange a deal with the company that plans to video-record the wedding day itself.

VIP Treatment

You could take the groom for a test drive in the car of his dreams or, if money is no object, hire a chauffeur-driven Rolls Royce for the evening. Then use a ticket agency to obtain tickets for an historical play or opera, Ascot, the races, or an equally popular match or show. This could be followed by drinks in a traditional gentleman's city business club. Alternatively an upmarket agency such as Crème de la Crème will get your group tickets for a concert, or theatre, with pre-show or interval drinks in the private rooms which are used by royalty and VIPs.

Wines and Views

You could arrange an evening on a wine company's premises or at a nearby hotel, calling in a wine company representative for a wine-tasting session. Those present could then give the groom a case of the wine he likes the most. Afterwards, if it is not a secret, you could show a video of the honeymoon destination, which the groom can then keep as a souvenir, so he will be able to get maximum enjoyment from trips around the honeymoon country.

Gourmet Banquets

Or you could arrange a dinner at a restaurant featuring the cuisine of the honeymoon country, dining on specialities not normally on the menu. These dishes must be ordered for your group several days in advance. Again this enables the groom to be better prepared to enjoy his honeymoon. The menu can be kept by the groom as a souvenir, signed by all the guests. You might like to order a vintage wine, champagne, or port, or two or three different wines from the country, and ask the wine waiter to describe them.

Live Entertainers

If you want live entertainment, the most personalized songs will come from a revue put on by the groom's own friends, a sort of amateur 'This is Your Life', with a few key guests arriving one by one, from the old school, previous workplace, or home town. All you need is a big banner, unfurled when the groom arrives, half a dozen photos borrowed from his mother and stuck in one of those magnetic page albums, a microphone, and a Polaroid camera. If you can get a few accessories, such school caps, football team or college scarves, and the words of the old school song, so much the better.

You could also try phoning one or more of the groom's distant friends, or an old school headmaster, or the teacher of the subject at which the groom was most successful. Ask if the friend or teacher remembers John, or whoever, and record the reply on a telephone answering machine. Make sure it is on the start of a new tape so you can locate it easily.

Your guests may include some talented amateur actors or singers who can make up amusing songs, strum guitars, mime to music, sing or dance.

Professionals

If you would rather spend money than time, live entertainers can be hired. Identify the groom's musical tastes, whether they are orchestral, opera, or jazz, or rock, reggae or pop. A live performance can be teamed with the gift of musical records or cassettes, or a stereo or CD player.

Make sure your act is good and reliable. I went to a party where the palm-reader failed to arrive because she was taken ill at the last moment. Whether she had seen this coming, I don't know, but the host had not!

You will also want to be sure that your entertainers can find their way across town to the venue through rush hour and arrive at the right time. Both the agent and you need to have their phone numbers at the location they are leaving from. You also need a note of the agency's phone number. Phone on the morning of the day to confirm. Then if they have forgotten, double-booked, blown up the transformer, got lost on the motorway, or fallen ill – you will be surprised at the comical excuses – you will have time to arrange something else. It is always a good idea to have a back-up of disco music, video tape or other entertainment just in case they fail to turn up on time. Avoid engaging unknown dubious entertainers. What sounds like a funny strip act might degenerate into an unsuitable audience involvement rugger scrum in which the guests lose half their clothes. Anyone who wakes up next day unable to remember what happened will image the worst happened to everybody else, though not to himself.

To ensure that you are booking a professional and acceptable act, try to engage a group which has been recommended and go to see them perform elsewhere first. If you want a particular singer or comedian, make sure that your arrangement with the company specifies this.

You cannot prevent the lead singer falling ill, but you can make it clear that you expect the group to consist of those you have met and not others using the same name. I had a particularly bad experience with wedding photographers which you could learn from. I booked a wedding photographer whose work I liked and with whom I had rapport. In fact I chose between two companies on the basis of this man's personality. However, the extrovert man who made the presentation to me and showed me his work was merely the rep on this occasion. More bookings for other weddings reached him for the wedding day and he sent someone else to take the wedding photos.

Dinner Shows

A less original but safer approach is to visit a gourmet ethnic restaurant or supper club which has public performances on stage. A well-known restaurant could be chosen, or one with a particularly attractive menu which is worth framing, or a restaurant which specializes in dinner shows such as flamenco dancing, Indian dancing, or Middle Eastern belly dancing. If you want something different, there are restaurants specializing in magic or medieval banquets.

STAG PARTY SPEECHES

When you hold a stag party in a private room at a restaurant, this is a good place to have some after dinner speeches and to present a gift to the groom. Some suggested speeches appear in the companion volume to this book, *Wedding Speeches & Toasts*.

The general tone of the best man's speech is a humorous one. Relate how the groom spent his time as a single man. Recall his achievement and cleverness, and unaccountable rare moments of stupidity. What are the qualities of the perfect married man? Does he possess them? The bride to be seems very charming. Has she made a wise choice? Look forward to the enormous improvements which could be made in him. And express fears about the occasional disappointments that will occur, when his bride attempts to change things! Finally extend the good wishes of yourself and all those present, and give him the gift which you trust will assist his new life, and contribute to the happiness of him and his new wife.

If you have had an evening out on the town, the whole group can see the groom home safely and make the presentation either at his home, or at the best man's home *en route*.

Assuming that the groom is making a speech in reply, take along a tape recorder. You can then put together a tape of the stag party speeches, adding the wedding day speeches later.

MAN TO MAN CHATS

The married best man, usher, or father may take this opportunity to advise the groom on marriage conduct and bedroom behaviour. Advice from different sources – proverbs, for instance – tends to conflict.

HEN PARTIES

While all this is going on it is only fair that the bride-to-be should be gathering with her girlfriends for a similar hen party organized by the Maid of Honour or Matron of Honour. If you are collecting photos from the boys' bachelor party, combine them with photos from the girls' hen party in the wedding book.

Girls should perhaps beware of trying to turn the tables on the boys by calling in a male stripper. One best man informed the groom who, when he heard of this plan, turned up in disguise and did a strip show, finally revealing all – including his identity, to the horror of the bride!

JOINT BACHELOR PARTIES

If there is a best girl, rather than having her organize a bachelor boys' party, hold a combined party for the singles. In a private house you can have the girls in one room and the boys in another. Or at a restaurant have a boys' table and a girls' table.

This is a last chance for everyone to contribute 'My mother's ten rules for a happy marriage,' and 'My father's ten rules for a happy marriage.' The rules which no longer apply – such as grandparents' advice to your mother and father when they married, will raise a few laughs. You could even have two opposing speakers, as in a debate.

If the party is held at home start with practical demonstrations such as 'How to make hospital corners on beds; cakes, biscuits, and meals made in ten minutes'.

When meeting in a restaurant swap lists and present a book of tips such as: 'What to do if the car won't start'; 'How to be sure you never lose your doorkey.' Later you might discuss how to avoid arguments; and how to keep him/her happy. Details of American bachelor parties are given on page 65.

PRE-WEDDING PLANS

For some best men there is a lull until the days immediately before the wedding. However, a large wedding with many attendants requires forward planning. Even the calmest wedding creates a flurry of activity and excitement in the last few days.

DUTIES DURING THE ENGAGEMENT

First the best man and ushers will be invited to a family dinner or the engagement party to meet the family.

Meeting the Bride

If you cannot think of anything else to say you can admire the ring, and tell the bride how you know the groom, and what a good choice they have both made. Since you are aiding the groom in organizing his side of the wedding, it is worthwhile finding out his bride's taste in music, clothes, colours, food, furnishing (you will be buying them a wedding present) and anything else which might be relevant.

Meeting the Bride's and Groom's Parents

Naturally you will express pleasure at the forthcoming marriage and say how pleased you are to be part of the wedding party. The bride's parents who pay for the wedding will be making decisions as to the number of guests and ushers.

Meeting the Ushers

The best man has overall charge and he directs the chief usher. A meeting is usually held at which he briefs the ushers. They have three chief areas of concern: clothes, church seating plans, and transport.

Wedding Clothes

The best man will be supervising fittings for either

formal and informal wedding clothes, co-ordinating outfits and accessories, in a style which establishes them all as members of the wedding group, but distinguishes them from the groom. A truly energetic best man will investigate all the clothes hire firms and locate one which has a convenient location, a wide choice, and reasonable prices. The best man may even negotiate for the groom to get complimentary clothes hire if he is bringing them the business of, for example, the hire of six ushers' outfits. Major hire companies have leaflets showing which accessories go with which formal outfits.

Black, white and grey men's suits and accessories will go with most colours the bridesmaids might choose. A heavy black will look better against strong colours in the girls's dresses, while pale grey offsets the paler pastels, so make a note that you must discuss the girls' colour schemes after the bride has decided.

Preliminary Seating Plans
Detailed seating plans of the church cannot be made until the numbers of guests and their relationships to the bride and groom are known. However, the best man can make a rough plan. The ushers should be given the basic rule to remember, to seat the bride's family on the left and the groom's on the right, which echoes the bride's and groom's position as they progress down the aisle.

Transport
The best man must check hire car costs and advise the groom. The car which brings the bride to the church, transfers the bride and groom to the reception, and then takes them to the hotel or airport can be one car hired for the day, driven by the best man. (Why not? It saves money. And although it takes time and trouble, the best man might enjoy the pleasure of driving a Rolls Royce.) Rolls Royce produce a booklet on the correct behaviour of a chauffeur driving a Rolls, which includes the wearing of driving gloves and opening car doors.

Alternatively a chauffeur-driven car can be ordered for each segment of the journey. If a car is hired for a minimum of one hour but the distance between the bride's home and the church is very short, the best man could arrange for the chauffeur to take the bridal couple for a spin in the Rolls Royce on the way.

Alternatives to the Rolls Royce are a Daimler, a stretch limousine, a tandem bicycle, or a helicopter for departure from the hotel where the wedding reception is held to the airport. If the bridal couple are marrying abroad there are many locations where horse-drawn carriages or Surreys are popular.

Hire company addresses can be found in the yellow pages of local phone books, or in advertisements in bridal magazines, or motoring magazines. Obviously you must remember to inform the hire company that the car is required for a wedding, so that the appropriate white ribbon can be placed on the bonnet.

The wedding party cars can be Rolls Royces, some years and models being more expensive than others. If you cannot get this year's model, you might go to the other extreme and choose a vintage car. Horses and carriages can be hired.

It is a good idea to suggest to the bride's mother that when guests telephone her she should check how they intend to reach the church and reception. Drivers can be sent maps indicating routes and parking. Those without transport can be put in touch with others coming from their area. Elderly relatives can be collected by others, or a note can be made to ensure that one of the ushers transports them from the church to the reception.

If guests speak foreign languages find out who can translate, and arrange for their mode of transport from the church to reception to be organized in advance. You don't want to be standing outside the church on the day trying to find out whether a silent, smiling Japanese lady has transport to the reception, and whether she has indeed been invited to the reception – a delicate question, even without the language difficulties.

Gifts

The gifts to the bride and groom will depend on the finances of the best man and ushers, whether the couple already have separate homes, and whether they badly need any major items such as bedding or curtains. Maybe they already have two sets of crockery, and do not need more, but cannot afford to re-carpet their new home, in which case a large rug might be welcome.

Paperwork

An older groom may wish to take charge of most of the practical details. But a younger one might rely on the assistance of an older brother to organize the paperwork. A groom who is arriving from abroad, or has heavy commitments to work or study, may also rely heavily on the best man. To prepare for the wedding there are applications for marriage licences, arrangements to meet the minister, and enquiries about the costs of the church service.

Honeymoon Advice

A budget must be made for the honeymoon, investigating possible honeymoon locations and comparing package tour prices. The groom will have to make reservations for the honeymoon transport and hotel, booking a honeymoon bedroom suite, and ordering extras such as champagne on arrival. The best man may have to chase up tickets which are not delivered, collect them and keep them safe, and confirm the flight.

The best man may be able to advise on the suitability of transport, hotels and bedrooms. Cruise ships and trains rarely have double beds, and package tours frequently give twin bed rooms. The best man might suggest that the groom tells the hotel he is on honeymoon and requires a double bed, or books a honeymoon suite with a double or four-poster bed.

There are numerous guides to UK locations. Local tourist boards can suggest hotels which have honeymoon suites, including the budget options such as bed and breakfast places with four-posters.

If the groom cannot afford any of this, the groom and ushers could club together and pay for the bride and groom to spend a night at a hotel with a honeymoon suite, or buy a couple of curtain rails and a curtain and, aided by the chief bridesmaid, rig up an improvised four-poster at home.

If the honeymoon is to be abroad, allow at least six weeks to order passports, visas, and vaccinations – which may have to be administered in two batches at widely spaced intervals.

Insurance

The best man should allocate a safe place, such as a body belt, or an inner pocket which buttons down or closes in the suit he is hiring, for keeping the bride's ring and the groom's suitcase keys. Car keys and doorkeys should also be kept safely. A key-ring can be attached by a black ribbon to an inside pocket so the keys can be extracted quickly, and never put down and lost. A set of duplicate keys can be given to the head usher, if the best man holds the main set. The best man could keep duplicate keys if the groom has the originals. Insurance can be taken out to cover possible loss of the ring, luggage and honeymoon holiday expenses, and the wedding itself.

It is also worthwhile checking on insurance policies to see whether items in the best man's care are covered by his household insurance, whether the policy for the bride's and groom's new home will cover presents delivered there before they move in, and whether clothing and wedding presents on display at the wedding reception are protected by insurance.

Receipts for deposits, dry cleaning receipts, and claim tickets for hired clothing and hire cars must be kept.

Speech
The best man should prepare his own speech, if necessary advise the groom on speechmaking, and keep a duplicate copy of the groom's speech. Make careful note of the spelling of family names, nicknames, titles of the family, friends and ministers or other VIPs who you or the groom should mention in your speeches.

Your library and bookshop will have many books on speechmaking. My companion volume to this one deals with wedding speeches and toasts in detail.

Sample speeches are given on pages 48–50.

Entertaining the Groom Before the Wedding
The stag party is never held the night before the wedding in case the groom ends up with a hangover. But the best man may need to keep the groom happily and harmlessly occupied while the bride-to-be is busy with wedding preparations. If the groom is saving up for all those wedding expenses, he might need to stay at home with the best man sharing a drink from the off licence, rather than spending money on expensive rounds of drinks in bars and pubs. The night before the wedding you might like to hear the groom rehearse his speech.

NEAR THE DAY
Helping to calm the groom's pre-wedding nerves is one of the tasks, best achieved by unflappability, good organization and careful attention to detail. Giving advice will be your pleasurable task if you are older and more experienced or already married.

In addition to hiring and returning his own morning dress the best man will collect the groom's. He should keep two telephone and address lists, one in his pocket and one taped by the telephone at home, giving the contact numbers for all major participants, relatives, ushers and other attendants, church, minister, caterer, hire car company, jeweller, and travel agent.

Finalizing Seating Plans in the Church

Visit the church when no wedding or service is taking place so that you can draw up a pew plan. Then make a seat plan, filling in the names or status of guests, e.g. bride's mother. Pew cards can be made for reserved seats. You need to be clear about the seating of divorced parents (see pages 39–40).

Wedding Rehearsal

A dry run or dress rehearsal can be held for the attendants, checking that you know when to produce the ring, where you will be standing, and when you will be speaking. Obtain copies of the church service for the groom, the bride, and yourself and other attendants.

You may want to do a dry run for the groom in your living room. He should have his clothes laid and ready and try them on in advance in front of you. That way you can check he isn't missing a collar-stud, wearing odd socks or a pair which don't match the shoes, or shoes which need new heels. The groom may go to church with the bride and watch another wedding the week before their own ceremony to see how it is done.

It is also handy to gather with the groom and ushers and look at some family photographs so that on the day you will instantly and enthusiastically recognize the bride's grandmother, stepfather, her real father, and other important people who need to be greeted and seated.

THE WEDDING DAY

Careful planning should make for a smooth-running and happy day. This is the day when the bride and groom are like king and queen with nothing to do except relax, smile and be joyful.

GETTING READY

Probably everybody will wake up early. But you should set two alarms to get yourself up, perhaps a clock plus a telephone alarm call. Then phone the groom. After that call at his home and help him dress. Take spare studs. Check that he has his marriage licence handy. Phone the ushers to ensure that they arrive at the church one hour in advance of the ceremony.

Parking

Earlier this century when few people owned cars the ushers were responsible for organizing hire car transport for all the guests. Nowadays it is only the wedding party itself which arrives at the church in grand hire cars. Most guests drive themselves to the wedding and need help with directions and parking. Some of the guests may need help finding transport to the church, and to the reception, and cars may be hired to meet particular trains.

When there is a car park near the church but no attendant, one of the ushers must remove any chain barrier and then direct into the car park the wedding guests arriving by car. Spaces should be reserved for some or all of the wedding party cars, unless they can be left in the road immediately outside the church without obstructing traffic. In city locations shoppers and passers-by looking for parking places can be courteously re-directed to other nearby public car parks.

A NO PARKING sign may be obtained from the church or one can be made to prevent shoppers from parking too near the church door where the bride's car will be drawing up.

The Church Decorations
The ushers should arrive at the church about one hour in advance in case any of the guests arrive early. If the best man has given the pew cards to the chief ushers these can be placed on the pews to reserve seats for important people. When the ushers arrive the flowers will probably already be arranged around the altar or wedding canopy, or the florist might be making the finishing touches. If by any chance the expected flowers are not ready or seem insufficient the chief usher should phone the bride's mother or florist.

Ushers' Duties
If the weather is wet or snowy, the ushers must take large umbrellas with them to the church and one or more ushers should open car doors, hold umbrellas overhead and escort guests into the church so they do not get wet. Similarly when guests leave they must escort them back to the cars.

Those ushers who know most of the guests should greet them and direct other ushers to lead the guests to their seats. The immediate family are identified by their buttonholes or corsages.

The family will be given the seats nearest the front with a good view of the ceremony. The bride's mother and the groom's mother will normally have been given corsages earlier in the day so they can arrive wearing them, especially the bride's mother who arrives at the last moment. The ushers may be distributing the flowers to them or other guests. Sometimes a flower is given from a huge basket of flowers to everyone arriving. But the wedding group always wear different flowers so they can be identified.

The groom and best man may wait seated in the front right hand pew (Christians in USA) or stand, (Christians in UK and Jewish). Those taking part in the ceremony require seats reserved in the front row – including the best man himself who will sit down after handing over the ring.

Other guests may be colleagues, neighbours, or friends. Those guests who are not known by the ushers are asked, 'Friends of the bride or groom?' The bride's friends sit on the left. The groom's sit on the right. Ushers should hand out order of service sheets, and prayer books to guests as they arrive.

In theory those arriving first should go to the far end of the pew so that others can get in without pushing past. In practice the early arrivals may take the aisle seats with the best view on a first come first served basis, tenaciously guarding their places by stepping out into the aisle to let the latecomers take the inside seats. If there seems to be any disagreement pending, the ushers can quickly move the latecomer to a second aisle seat further back.

Ladies with strapless dresses or other clothing unsuitable for church can be tactfully advised to keep their coats on during the service. Where the church requires men to wear hats or ladies to cover their hair with lace headcoverings these can be distributed. If men and women are sitting separately, as in a synagogue, newly arrived persons who are unaware of this fact should have it explained to them.

Seating Precedence

Generally the closest family are given the seats nearest the front. Those partaking in the ceremony are given seats in the front row so that they can quickly and easily leave the seats and return to them.

If the bride's mother has remarried but her first husband, the bride's father, takes part in the ceremony he sits next to the bride's mother. The bride's stepfather, her mother's second husband, sits behind. Do not seat him alongside his rival, nor on the other side of the bride's mother as if the two men are competing for her attention. Even if the stepfather is paying for the wedding, the bride's own father may be the person who is closest to her and chosen to take part in the ceremony.

If the bride's mother and stepfather are hosts and taking part in the ceremony, the bride's father and his second wife will be given seats in the row behind. Apart from saving them the embarrassment of sitting next to each other, this saves the guests confusion. The wording of the wedding invitation itself should have indicated to both ushers and guests who the hosts are.

Seats near the front need to be saved so that small children who take part in the procession as bridesmaids and pages are not obliged to remain standing throughout the service. A seat must be allocated to a nanny or childminder if the child's mother is partaking in the service.

Families with babies or small children can be seated near a door at the back so they can make a quick exit if necessary. A few spaces near the back should be saved so that late arrivals can slip in unobtrusively. Similarly spaces should be saved for those with sticks or wheelchairs who do not wish to negotiate long distances. However, be sure that spaces with obscured views of the ceremony are not allotted when other places affording a better view are left free. Try to ensure that tall people with large hats are not seated in front of children or small people, but further back.

Ushers' Behaviour and Deportment

The ushers should all be wearing carnations of the same colour, different to the colour of the one worn by the groom. The bride can be presumed to know who's who. But this system is a great help to short-sighted great-uncles trying to sort out which of the twin boys or similar brothers is getting married, and the bride's mother's friends from the shop or office – who know neither bride nor groom. It makes sure the photographer doesn't keep photographing the head usher instead of the groom. If the ushers' carnations match the colour of the bridesmaid's dresses or flowers, e.g. pink, and the groom's carnation matches that of the bride's dress or flowers, e.g. white, it is clear to onlookers who is partnering whom.

The ushers should not engage in long conversations with each other or friends, ignoring and delaying arriving guests. If a fond aunt tries to block the doorway and engage in extended conversation say something like, 'Aunty, let me find you a seat. . . . I must go back now but I look forward to talking to you later.' If the aunt has arrived well in advance she can be introduced to the person sitting next to her which will deflect her from distracting the busy usher.

The ushers should be calm, dignified and poised, not dash around looking agitated. They should also stand upright and not lounge against door pillars or recline on the sides of pews. Since they are conspicuous and likely to appear on camera during the day, they should remember not to jingle coins in their pockets, and avoid stroking their hair, and moustaches, lips and beards. When they are not occupied they can stand with their hands folded together, looking outward from the doorway to meet the eyes of approaching guests.

When several guests arrive together the chief usher might escort somebody important such as an elderly grandmother. If there is a group, the usher takes the oldest or most important person to lead the way. He offers his right arm to a single lady or to support anybody needing assistance.

At any time during the day when the best man, bride's mother or photographer seem unduly busy, an usher who is not occupied might offer to help, asking, 'Is there anything I can do for you?'

BEST MAN'S ARRIVAL AT CHURCH

The best man accompanies the groom to the church. In the olden days he would have been with the groom, theoretically to be ready to defend the groom. Nowadays this custom is followed so the groom knows the best man will 'get me to the church on time'. They may enter together from an east-right hand door and stand waiting for the bride. The best man stands to the right of the groom and slightly behind him. The organist plays quiet music.

The bride's mother arrives last before the bride, with the smallest bridesmaids and pageboys, who are often her grandchildren. The only exception to this is when the HM the Queen attends, in which case she is last to arrive before the bride.

An usher waits by the church door for the arrival of the bride and informs the church choir so that the organist can strike up with 'Here comes the bride' or another appropriate tune which will arouse the attention of the guests in the church, and cause them to rise to their feet, stop talking, and look towards the bride.

Preceded by the minister and choir, the bride enters on the arm of her father or whoever is giving her away. It could be a stepfather or uncle if her father is deceased, sick, abroad or unable to attend. After she has entered the church an usher shuts the church doors and ensures that nobody enters and walks down the aisle in the middle of the ceremony. It is useful to be equipped with a spare handkerchief in case the bride or bride's mother bursts into tears.

Safeguarding the Ring

The best man has charge of the ring given by the groom to the bride. Many couples have his and her wedding rings and the best man may be entrusted with both. If he is right-handed for maximum convenience he must keep the ring (or rings) in his right hand pocket, or inside left pocket, and take out the gold or platinum band when required. Jewellers usually supply a ring box with a new ring. If this is too bulky for the best man's inside pocket, small zippered or buttoned purses are made for jewellery. A valuable heirloom ring or secondhand ring usually has a protective box. A ring which is not new may need cleaning before the ceremony. A jeweller will advise on how to clean it without damaging it or leaving marks.

The best man should not take the ring out of the box and carry it loose in his pocket. It can drop through a hole in his pocket into the jacket lining, or gather fluff inside the pocket. It is possible for the best man to transfer the ring into his hands just before the ceremony starts and wear the ring on his little finger so as to be able to produce it immediately.

The ring is placed upon the Bible held by the minister. The ring will be placed on the bride's fourth finger of her left hand by the groom. The best man may have taken it upon himself to remind the groom that in some European countries rings are worn on the other hand. Catholics follow a more elaborate ritual for placing the ring on the bride's hand. In Jewish ceremonies the ring may be placed on the bride's middle finger.

If by chance the ring rolls off under the pews during the ceremony, you do not want the bride and groom and ushers crawling around on hands a knees hunting for it, while the minister and guests wait anxiously. The best man should produce another ring. The ceremony then continues. When the proceedings are over the best man or chief usher should retrieve the ring after the guests have moved and it is easier to find.

After the minister has blessed the ring and passed it to the groom, the best man may sit down.

AFTER THE CEREMONY

The Register

The register is signed by the minister or registrar together with the bride and groom and two witnesses, who can be the maid of honour and best man, or two of the parents. If the minister has covered the register showing the bride's signature, which is in her maiden name, do not try to remove the cover. He may be discreetly concealing some personal detail not known to others outside the family such as the fact that she is adopted, or was the daughter of her mother's previous marriage.

Settlement of Clergy Fees

Payments are made to the clergyman, choir, and bell-ringers. The groom sometimes gives their money to the best man the night before to minimize the amount of last minute activity on the day. The most discreet method is to place the money (notes or cheques) in envelopes. Each envelope should have the name of the recipient neatly written on the outside. This enables the best man to recall the names and say, 'Thank you Mr Brown,' and ensures you do not mix up the envelopes and give the wrong amounts. The envelopes should be sealed. The minister of the church is entitled to payment, even if another minister has taken part or all of the service.

The best man leaves the vestry to summon the bridal car and when he returns the bridal group gather for the Recession.

The Recession

It is bad form to try to enter the church interrupting the ceremony and an usher can ask latecomers to wait outside or until a suitable moment before entering. The usher should not lock the doors or obstruct anyone from entering, however, since this might be construed as forcing the bride to marry under duress, or preventing anyone with an objection to the marriage raising it. This is unlikely, but it is an important technical and legal point. Sometimes a latecomer or someone who has slipped out to the cloakroom manages to sneak into the back of a large church unobtrusively.

Generally the guests all wait to see the bride returning down the aisle on the arm of her new husband, but an official photographer may wish to leave ahead of them and fix up his tripod by the church steps.

The bride and groom walk back down the aisle. If it is a double wedding they are followed by the second bride and groom. The best man and the maid of honour or chief bridesmaid follow, together. Other ushers are paired with bridesmaids. Finally the parents of bride and groom bring up the rear.

The Guard of Honour
A guard of honour may consist of soldiers or other groups in uniform, sailors, RAF, police, nurses, Boy Scouts or Girl Guides. They are seated at the back so that they can leave fast to form a human archway with raised arms holding banners, flags, batons or swords through which the bride and groom emerge. You will want to arrange matters so that the photographers are ready to capture this moment promptly, and guests are briefly delayed in the church entrance hall or directed to other exits so they do not flood out of the church into the back of the group being photographed.

Church Photographs
The best man and head usher probably both wish to be in the photographs taken on the church steps. If necessary they can both be in one photograph, then take turns at being in the photographs while the other attends to the guests. After the photographs are taken in front of the church, the bride's parents and those who will be on the receiving line leave first so they can get to the reception hall ready to receive the first guests.

Organizing Transport to the Reception

The best man opens the door of the car (unless the chauffeur has done so) and sees the bride and groom into the car.

One usher should be at the car park exit, advising guests which way to turn into the road, suggesting the quickest route, and ensuring they have the address. Drivers with empty seats can be asked if they would mind taking those guests who do not have transport. One car is kept till last for the best man and the last usher, with an empty seat or two for any guest who is lost or left behind without transport.

An usher should go ahead to the reception car park to do the same there. A junior usher may be able to make himself useful at the hotel or hall directing the guests where to leave their coats, pointing out the toilets, the location of the hall, and acting as go-between and generally assisting the bride's mother. The usual system for cars is that the bride and groom go in the first car, then the bride's mother and groom's father, then the bride's father and bridegroom's mother, then the other attendants.

Retain hire cars or other transport at the reception location to enable the family and guests to return home from the reception.

More details about particular wedding ceremonies can be found in *Wedding Etiquette* by Margot Lawrence, also in this series.

PREPARING THE BEST MAN'S SPEECH

The best man makes a speech on behalf of the attendants. Its content varies according to the number of attendants, the nature of the previous speech and speeches, and who still needs to be toasted and thanked as hosts of the reception. Usually he concludes with a toast to the parents of the bride. But he may also toast the parents of the groom, particularly if they have shared the wedding costs, or if the majority of the guests are their relatives and friends.

When there have been several long speeches, or few and only brief ones, the best man's speech can be made to sound short, spontaneous, and sincere. But a confident, extrovert best man with a receptive audience can make a longer, humorous speech with personal anecdotes and jokes about the groom, and his favourite quotation or story – providing he has not told it to the family at a previous wedding. Speeches can be along the following lines, adapting anecdotes and compliments so that sufficient attention is focused on the person or persons you are toasting:

Brief reply to previous speaker's toast to bridesmaids:
'Thank you for your kind words. The bridesmaids and I have truly enjoyed this wonderful occasion, and will have many happy memories. (Add personal comment or anecdote on the pleasures of the date, the relationship of attendants to bride and groom, mention any assistance from the family – for example a relative may have made the bridesmaids' dresses; or refer to whether bridesmaids had ever been bridesmaids before.) It is now my pleasure to ask you to stand and raise your glasses and drink to the health of Steven and Sally (the bride's parents).'

Longer speech in reply to toast to bridesmaids:
'Thank you, Peter, for your kind words about the
bridesmaids and attendants. It has certainly been a
pleasure for all of us to take part in this wonderful
wedding day. The ushers and I have enjoyed escorting
the bridesmaids, and I know the dresses chosen by the
bride Anne and her mother Jane and the yellow flower
arrangements have attracted much favourable comment
from the guests here. (Pause for cries of, 'Here, here!')

'Our contribution has been an expression of the
happiness we feel at taking part in this joyful occasion.
Our hosts John and Jane have organized this event – the
practical details of the food and flowers, music and
dancing, everything that makes this day special, but in
reality everything they have done over the years to
educate and bring up Anne, our lovely bride, has led to
this perfect day. I would like you to stand and join the
bridesmaids and myself in drinking a toast to the health
and happiness of John and Jane. (Pause.) To John and
Jane.'

**Short speech for when there is a maid of honour but
no ushers or bridesmaids:**
'Thank you for your kind words. No-one knows better
than I how much the Maid of Honour, Lucinda, merits
your compliments and thanks. But for Lucinda and
myself ample repayment has been the pleasure of sharing
with you this wonderful occasion. We merely had the
enjoyable taks of assisting and helping to carry out the
design and plan for this wedding arranged by Anne's
parents Jane and John. I am sure that everyone present
here will want to stand and join Lucinda and myself in
proposing a toast to Jane and John. (Raise glass.) To
Jane and John.'

**Longer speech for when there are no ushers or
bridesmaids:**
'I have never been a best man before and had no idea

how much work it would entail. My duties have ranged from guarding the 24 carat gold ring for Anne as if my life depended upon it – which of course it did – to ... (add joking list of duties).

'Needless to say, these duties were all a great surprise to me, but also a great pleasure because John has been my friend for many years since (add personal details of when you met at school, tennis club, work or wherever).

'But my tasks were simple compared to the organization required by John and Jane who have created this most wonderful occasion, a truly splendid reception to celebrate the marriage of Anne and Mark, welcoming Mark and his parents Tony and Elizabeth to the family, and enabling us all to share their happiness. I would now like to ask you to drink a toast to the health of our hosts, John and Jane (bride's parents or other hosts). They are such charming hosts that I know they will also want you to raise your glasses to Tony and Elizabeth (bride-groom's parents). First, to John and Jane (sip champagne or wine), but also to their new family Tony and Elizabeth (sip again).'

Humorous speech when there are no bridesmaids or ushers:

'I have been a best man at many weddings. I warned Peter that on previous occasions I have lost the ring, left the honeymoon luggage at home – my home in (name distant suburb or next town). And once I even got everyone in their cars after the wedding at the church and then realized I had no way of getting myself to the reception.

'He didn't believe any of this. Peter is a very practical person. "You don't have to do anything," he said. "Just leave it all to Anne's mother. It will be all right on the day." And he was right. Her mother Jane, ably supported by her husband Mark, has created one of the most superb weddings I have ever attended – and I have been to many – but I think you will agree that (mention flower decorations or any impressive feature if there is one) she has created the perfect day – one which we will all remember. So I ask you to join me in standing and raising your glasses to drink a toast to our friends – Anne's parents and Peter's new in-laws, Jane and Mark. To Jane and Mark."

At weddings in America the best man proposes the toast to the bride and groom. For more details on alternative ceremonies see pages 60–73.

Notes on helping the groom with his speech are in the chapter on pre-wedding preparations. The best man keeps a duplicate copy of his own speech and the groom's, so as to have it ready for the delivery on the day, and afterwards for reference.

AT THE RECEPTION

WELCOME SIGNS

The house or hall where the reception is held should be made as easy to find as possible. Check that there is a sign with the hall or hotel name at the turning off the main road and the entrance to the driveway. If possible indicate that the wedding reception is held there by adding some wedding symbol such as carnations and balloons with slogans such as congratulations.

Have the cloakrooms and toilets checked earlier in the day. Management should fix missing locks, replace missing light bulbs, stock up with spare toilet rolls, add flowers, spray the Ladies with perfumed air freshener and generally make the place welcoming. The bride will be unable to get into a small cubicle if she is wearing a dress with a long train. Even if she is not staying the night at the hotel, they may make available a bedroom with *en suite* bathroom where you can leave the honeymoon luggage, secure wedding presents delivered on the way, and where the bride and groom can change into their going away clothes.

The groom's, best man's and ushers' top hats and gloves may be left in a cloakroom or left in the bedroom used as a changing room. The best man can take charge of the groom's hat so that the groom can go straight to the receiving line.

RECEIVING LINE

Compile a guest list to give to the toastmaster. Toast-masters usually have loud voices but if he requires a microphone, check it is in place and ask him to try it out and inform the management if it is not properly connected and adjusted. If there is no toastmaster, go through the names, checking how to pronounce them all. Announce the guests as they approach the receiving line.

Ushers should direct guests to drinks and chairs, make introductions and talk to anyone who is on their own. If you are having a wedding breakfast early in the day the drinks before the meal may be dispensed with.

TABLE SEATING

The seating for a wedding breakfast or dinner is as follows. The bride and groom sit together but their respective parents are separated. So the bride has her new husband on her right and her father on her left. The groom has his mother-in-law on his right; she has the groom's father on her right, the groom's father has the chief bridesmaid on his right; and the chief bridesmaid has the best man on her right. If there are several bridesmaids the best man is not alone on the far right but has another bridesmaid next to him. Going to the left of the bride's father are the bridegroom's mother, and usher, bridesmaid, usher, bridesmaid, alternating male and female along the table.

An alternative system is to have the younger people on another table. If children who have not been invited to the sit-down meal are arriving immediately after it, they can join the younger people, be sent to their own parents, or can fill in empty spaces left by 'no shows'. But as it is not pleasant to sit next to an empty chair for a long period, caterers can be asked to remove the chair and place-setting from places set up for those who are certain not to appear.

CAKE CUTTING

The timing of the cake cutting will depend on the size and duration of the meal. When the cake will be a dessert, or will follow dessert with coffee after a light meal, the best man or master of ceremonies announces the cake cutting which is then followed by speeches.

However, if the meal is large and a long evening of dancing follows the coffee and speeches, the best man will call the bridal group back to the tables and summon the photographer for the cake cutting ceremony. The toastmaster might make the announcement after the best man has gathered everyone together or the best man may use the microphone belonging to the band if there is dancing. The cake is then passed around to accompany tea and coffee served later, with light sandwiches or Danish patries for those who arrived after dinner, are still hungry, or do not like wedding cake.

The ushers should see that a drink is taken to the band. Wedding cake will be saved for those unable to attend the wedding and the caterer will put it in a box at the end of the evening. It may be too heavy for the bride's mother to carry, in which case the best man or head usher can carry it to the car for her.

The parents of small children not invited to the wedding may gather up leftover petit-fours. However, rather than leaving the guests to wrap up oddments surreptitiously, the ushers and attendants could be encouraged to offer the petit-fours to guests who are likely to want to take them home, presented in silvery wrapping paper or teeny baskets. The European custom (especially in Italy) is for voile bags of sugared almonds in pink, white and silver to be given to the guests.

SPEECHES

Speeches begin after the guests have finished eating. Waiters should be instructed to fill wineglasses ready for the toasts. Announcements are made by the toastmaster or best man, 'Ladies and Gentlemen, you may now smoke,' and 'Pray silence for (name of speaker) who will propose a toast to (name)'.

After checking the microphone, the toastmaster or best man introduces the first speaker, and in due course the other speakers. Speeches should be delivered calmly with a confident, happy manner. Ushers can admit latecomers between the speeches, greeting these guests with enthusiasm and finding them something to eat and drink.

TELEGRAMS

Telegrams may have arrived from relatives and friends overseas, those who are old or living far away, and those who are obliged to work on the wedding day. There may also be telegrams from groups of friends belonging to social organizations, school, college, or work colleagues.

If the best man is the groom's father, or the older brother who is head of the family, and wants to orchestrate every detail of the wedding to make it a wonderful occasion uniting the family from far corners of the globe, he might have reminded distant brothers and cousins to send telegrams, and suggested quotations which he is not using in his own speech.

The master of ceremonies, if there is one, must be handed the telegrams by the best man, who can sort them into order of importance, starting with the nearest or oldest relative, ending with telegrams from friends or if possible an amusing telegram.

If there is no master of ceremonies the best man reads the telegrams. Large numbers of telegrams would take time to read. Those from nearest relatives can be read in full. Others can be summarized, 'John Smith sends his best wishes'. Afterwards the telegrams should be kept safely by the best man and returned to the bride's mother, or sent to the couple's new home. The best man can keep the telegrams in a large white envelope labelled Wedding Telegrams to (bride's and groom's names) so that they do not get crumpled. The bride may wish to stick them into a wedding book with a copy of the wedding invitations, photographs, cutting from the local newspaper, and wedding menu.

Sending telegrams is traditional. But if a relative has thought to send a cassette with a message instead it might be worthwhile playing that – remember to bring along a cassette recorder.

If many relatives cannot attend, perhaps because the bride and groom's families live in different countries, the best man could have arranged to have a brief video made of a group of relatives or friends on an army base in Gibraltar, faraway Hong Kong, Singapore or Australia, saying how glad they are to be able to speak, that they send their good wishes, and that they are thinking of the bride and groom and opening a bottle of champagne.

The video should be rewound so it is at the start of the tape. The VCR and TV must be set up in advance, with a dry run to ensure all the plugs and switches are on. If the VCR is taken to a hotel or hall, the best man should make sure that it has been gathered up at the end of the evening, complete with all leads, and the tape, which should be clearly labelled with the subject and the bride's address, to guard against loss.

DANCING

Should the best man dance with the bride? Yes, but only after she has danced with the groom and her father. The best man should dance with the chief bridesmaid if she is single and unattached, although if she is engaged to be married he would not monopolize her. He does not have to dance with all the bridesmaids. That is the ushers' job, though it would be a nice gesture to dance once with each of them, especially if he sees one of them sitting alone.

The ushers need not confine their attention to the bridesmaids, but might offer to dance with any of the lady guests, especially those who are tapping their feet, strumming the table, clapping, or swinging their heads in time to the music, without having yet been invited to dance.

Elderly guests stuck near a loud band can be moved, or the band can be asked to play more quietly, or to play a slow number. Ladies who are sitting with backs to the band, clearly not interested in the music, might welcome a few minutes, conversation instead. Girls or women who are dancing together might be pleased to be introduced to a couple of male dance partners. At the end of the dance or dances the usher or best man should thank the lady and escort her back to her seat.

Any young lady who is stuck with her family on a far table can be invited to join the young people when some of them get up to dance and vacate seats. Similarly teenage children who arrive after the dinner because they were not invited to the full meal can be asked to join the other youngsters. Whether or not the best man dances with all the single lady guests depends on the size of the gathering. It is an option. He should certainly see that no lady is left sitting alone after all the others on her table have got up to dance.

PHOTOGRAPHS

The best man might organize some photographs to be taken out of doors before the meal while there is still good light outside. He will have to retrieve the top hats and gloves if they have previously been taken away. He should summon the bridesmaids and get the ushers to pose with them for photographs. Also he should find grandparents, step-parents, siblings, children, and other VIPs for photographs.

DEPARTURE FOR HONEYMOON

The best man should know the groom's flight and destination but keep the information secret.

He should watch the clock or set a timer on his watch to ensure that the bride and groom do not miss their flight. He should remind the bride and groom when to change clothes, have the going away outfits ready, and collect the wedding clothes in a protective container with the hire documents.

The best man who has been keeping the documents now hands over the honeymoon travel tickets and passports and he reminds the groom to check that no vital documents have been left in the pockets of the wedding suit or left at home. The best man then ensures that the going away car arrives, with Just Married adornments. Phone for a hotel porter or despatch ushers to carry the honeymoon luggage to the car. Call the family to wave goodbye to the honeymoon couple and clear a path through the crowd so the couple can reach the car. Give the groom the car keys, or drive the couple to the airport. Return the groom's car to the couple's new home and return to the scene of the reception.

Alternatively he could drive the couple to their honeymoon hotel. Sign in for them. Check that champagne is waiting for them on ice in their bedroom. Check that luggage is in the room or send up the bellboy immediately with the luggage.

If the couple are staying the night at the same hotel as the one where the reception is held, you can arrange to have leftover food and drink kept for the couple, as a midnight feast or breakfast in bed.

CLEARING UP

Return to the reception hall and collect telegrams, wedding presents and any found items. Report any lost items to caterers, cleaning staff, and hotel management.

INFORMAL WEDDINGS

A best man is still usually required at an informal wedding, though if there are no bridesmaids, and/or not more than fifty guests, it is not necessary to have ushers.

The informal wedding is less demanding in terms of finance and etiquette. However, it offers more opportunity for ingenuity in finding ways to make the occasion personal and special. The do-it-yourself wedding is great fun.

PREPARING THE CAR

The best man should clean the car. He may have to take his own car or the groom's to a carwash. Fill the car up with petrol. Clean out the car interior. Clean the car boot and if it is dirty line it with old cleaned carpet. Place a large golfing umbrella in the boot just in case it rains. Borrow a big umbrella if you do not have one, or buy one from an umbrella specialist, or the lost and found departments of the London Underground. A large black umbrella can be decorated with white or silver decorations. A large white one could be decorated with flowers to match the bride's outfit and used as a parasol if it is sunny. Or simply tie a couple of white balloons to the handle.

CLOTHES

Clean your shoes, and have your suit cleaned – or hire one or even treat yourself to a new one. Buy a new shirt. Select a tie and socks.

PHOTOGRAPHS

Bring a camera and some spare film. See if a local camera shop stocks cheaper film in bulk.

AT THE CHURCH

Drive the groom to the church. Accompany the maid of honour, if there is one, in the Recession. Drive the couple back home or to the reception. If they are going away, drive them to the airport and plan to collect them on their return.

THE RECEPTION

At the reception gather the guests for the cake-cutting and group photos. Remind the groom to thank his in-laws personally. Have some spare alcoholic drink available. Keep spare coins for phone boxes and cash for emergency purchases.

Buy the first round of drinks at the bar. Organize a surreptitious whip-round for more drink, take-away food, or a gift for the couple.

When they leave for the honeymoon, remind the bride and groom to phone home to absent relatives such as divorced parents. Fetch coats for the guests. Check that everyone has a lift home. Or persuade them to club together for a minicab. Walk people who live nearby home.

Finally clean the Just Married sign off the car belonging to yourself or the groom.

DUTIES FOR DIFFERENT CEREMONIES AND CUSTOMS

When you are attending a wedding in another country or one hosted by the bride's parents who are from another country, you should be prepared for the customs of their weddings. If you are involved in planning a wedding in the UK at which the bride's family from abroad will be attending, you need to make sure that the incoming best man or ushers know how our customs differ. It would be a nice gesture to incorporate some of the rituals which will be familiar to them.

Most weddings in the UK take place in church (not on Sunday) or in a register office (not on Saturday afternoons or Sunday), or in a synagogue (not on Saturday or religious holidays). Quaker and Jewish weddings can take place at any hour and in any location and Jewish weddings can take place out of doors.

CHURCH OF ENGLAND WEDDINGS

In England marriage requires banns being called announcing that the wedding will take place and requesting anyone who knows any reason why it should not to come forward. This is done in the church where the marriage will take place and usually also in the churches of the parishes where the bride and groom currently live, if they are in different areas. There is a fee for the publication of banns (making the announcements) and for the certificate of banns (certificate proving that this has been done). Further fees are charged for the marriage service and the marriage certificate issued at the wedding. The certificate can either be collected by you in person, or posted at additional cost. The organist and each member of the choir will also require a fee. Church fees are handed over before the ceremony.

An alternative to banns is a common licence. A special

licence can be acquired which will allow you to be married elsewhere, in a hospital for instance.

A marriage can take place in the Church of England if one partner is a member, i.e. has been baptised and christened in the Church of England. In Scotland you can be married at home or in a hotel. Details are obtainable from Scottish register offices. The important thing is to apply for the documentation in good time and for the groom to be resident a sufficient number of days wherever required.

ROMAN CATHOLIC WEDDINGS

Roman Catholic marriage ceremonies are of two types: the Rite of Marriage during Mass, and the Rite of Marriage outside of Mass. The former, more lengthy service, is most common where both partners are Catholics, whilst the latter is most common when a Catholic is marrying a non Catholic.

A lengthy period of preparation is required before a Catholic marriage, whether 'mixed' (Catholic and non Catholic) or not, as the two partners are instructed by their priest in the meaning of Catholic marriage and the necessary forms and dispensations are acquired. For further information, contact the Catholic Marriage Advisory Council, or consult your priest.

The best man, as in other marriage ceremonies, accompanies the groom and safeguards the ring or rings before handing these over to the priest at the correct time in the ceremony. Most commonly the best man and groom arrive at the church about 20 minutes before the bride and wait at the front right hand side of the church for the bride. An alternative Entrance Rite is for the best man, groom and bridesmaids to await the bride at the church door, where they are greeted by the priest. A procession to the altar then ensues, led by the priest and other officials, followed by the bride and groom, the best man, bridesmaids, and the parents of bride and groom.

When it is not possible for a couple to be married in a Roman Catholic church – when one partner is divorced, or not baptized for instance, there are a number of alternative options. A couple may be able to marry in a non-conformist church – the Methodist Church, the Baptist Church, The Society of Friends (Quakers), the Church of Scotland, and the United Reform Church, are all possible venues for a bride or groom who still has a living divorced spouse. Alternatively, it is quite popular for such couples to marry in a register office and then to receive a blessing from their local priest.

On some occasions, a marriage can take place in a Roman Catholic church with an Anglican priest/vicar taking part, or at an Anglican Church with a Roman Catholic priest assisting, providing that both ministers agree. Consult the Roman Catholic Directory.

ORTHODOX ETHNIC WEDDINGS

At schools and colleges you may make friends who practise other religions. It is a great honour to attend a wedding and find that your friend has included you among just half a dozen friends who are invited from outside the family and religious community.

It is a particular honour to be invited to an orthodox wedding. Even if the hosts are of your own religion, if you are from a liberal group you may be in for a few pleasant surprises.

Jewish Weddings

Jews can remarry in synagogue even if they were previously married in a synagogue provided the divorced partner will provide a 'Get' or religious document of release.

Pre-ceremony drinks and food are provided at some city weddings in the USA, not in the UK.

At orthodox ceremonies the party may go first to the rabbi's room or bride's room where the bride is veiled and the Hebrew marriage contract is signed with the best man as witness. The groom is supposed to see the bride without the veil before the marriage takes place to be sure he is not being married off to her less attractive sister.

The ushers may have to explain to non-Jewish guests that men entering the synagogue are expected to wear head-coverings, but non-Jews are not obliged to wear a prayer-shawl. It would be a thoughtful gesture to ensure that non-Jewish visitors have somebody Jewish next to them who can explain what will happen. At the most orthodox synagogues men and women sit separately. In ultra-orthodox communities women wear a head covering too. You do not kneel in a synagogue, but simply stand and sit when the others do.

Headcovering for guests is provided by the host. In the synagogue men wear headcovering and prayer shawls. Paper skullcaps called couples or kipot (Hebrew plural) may be provided on a table by the door for any guests who have forgotten theirs, or for non-Jewish friends. If you are not wearing a top hat as a member of the bridal party, you will probably want to wear your own more elaborate embroidered velvet couple. Get it out in advance and check that it is in good condition and does not need sewing, cleaning or ironing. If you want a new one they can be bought from Jewish shops specializing in religious gifts. You may need a hair grip to keep the hat on your hair.

During the ceremony, and when attending the synagogue the week beforehand, the groom may have to recite in Hebrew, and the best man might help him practise this in advance.

The orthodox seating tradition is for the bride's family to sit on the right but reform communities reverse this. There are four systems of procession. (Details in books obtainable from the Jewish Museum and Bookshop, London, which also runs a video about Jewish customs.) Under the canopy the best man stands on the left, behind or beside the groom.

Remind the groom that he has to place the ring on the bride's index or pointing finger – which is chosen so that she can show the ring to the witnesses. The ring must belong to the groom. So if the second ring is used because the real ring is too small or gets lost (see Troubleshooting guide) any extra inexpensive ring belonging to the groom would be acceptable – providing the bride accepts it. This would be better than a ring borrowed from his mother which she might decide to reclaim after giving it to him. The groom might want to carry a spare signet ring, or entrust it to the best man.

At the end of the ceremony the groom stamps on a glass and breaks it, symbolizing destruction of the temple, and remembering sorrow amidst joy. Another explanation for this ritual is that it symbolizes the irrevocability of the marriage. It is usual for the best man, ushers and guests to shout *mazel tov*, meaning good luck.

The Hebrew marriage document is signed after the ceremony at reform synagogues. The best man will hand over the fees including any travel expenses to the rabbi and cantor (singer) after the ceremony in a sealed envelope.

More details can be obtained by consulting Jewish books or encyclopaedias in British libraries at synagogues and universities.

At the wedding reception the best man does not stand in the receiving line. At the reception you may have to satisfy the more orthodox elderly guests as to whether their kosher food has been provided if the rest of the guests are not getting kosher food.

Muslim
Shoes are removed at the entrance to the mosque. Details are obtainable from Islamic centres and bookshops.

EUROPEAN VARIATIONS

The wedding car will not necessarily be decorated in the British manner in other countries of Europe. It could have a pink or white bow tied to the car radio aerial, and more bows tied to door handles and anything to which a bow can be attached.

French

The best man is called the *garçon d'honneur*. During the wedding reception the bride may expose the garter on her leg. The men in the audience shout out offers of money if she will raise the garter higher up the leg and lift her skirt to expose more leg. While perhaps the very richest families would not do this, for the average couple it is a popular way of obtaining money to make a better start in life and pay for the honeymoon and spending money. The immediate family and closest friends, such as the best man, will shout more often and louder, and offer larger denominations of money when the garter is very high up the thigh and the auction is more intense.

Greek Orthodox

Note the position the best man stands in church – slightly behind the groom because the best man has to change over the head-dress worn by the bride and groom which is swapped symbolically. The best man is invited to choose the bridal couple's child's name and will give presents to the child.

AMERICAN

In America a wedding rehearsal is held the day before the wedding and a rehearsal dinner is held the night before the wedding. The Bachelor Dinner is held two nights before the wedding, so that it takes place when everyone is in town. The day after the wedding a breakfast is held for the departing guests by the groom's family – no speeches here.

The groom wears one colour, perhaps a white tuxedo

to match the bride's white dress, while the best man wears another colour such as grey. Or the groom can wear light grey, the best man and ushers (also known as groomsmen) dark grey. The tuxedo is a dinner jacket – a 'regular' suit jacket or tails. Matching the jacket are white, black or grey grousers – sometimes grey with a stripe.

White shirts are standard wear, but coloured shirts were previously worn, with pink being popular. Swathes of black are appearing on sophisticated evening gowns for girls, so black jackets for their escorts' suits may make a comeback. Keep watching the advertisements in bridal magazines for the latest fashion. The ushers wear ties of the colour matching the bridesmaids' gowns – usually bow ties, possibly cummerbunds in the same colour, or sashes.

At a less formal wedding men wear a suit in black, white, tan or light grey. The white shirt may have many pleats down the front. An Ascot neckerchief, or cravat, might be worn.

Women wear three quarter length dresses. Short dresses are acceptable wear when the men are in tuxedos.

For a fancy wedding the groom wears a top hat and carries a cane, and sometimes the best man and all the ushers do so too, and the bridesmaids wear hats.

The Wedding Ceremony

After the guests are seated in church flower girls, age 4–8, enter first and strew rose petals, or hand a single rose or flower to the ladies. Then come the junior bridesmaids, age 12–15, then the bridesmaids, finally the bride.

Weddings can be arranged at numerous locations such as the wedding chapel on the moored hotel ship Queen Mary, in public parks, or in the gazebos by the fountains at rose gardens of theme parks and hotels. A house wedding can take place in which the procession goes down the stairs.

At a large wedding there may be a professional paid wedding organizer. The best man wears a gardenia; each usher has a carnation in his buttonhole. This is called a 'boutonnière'. In a church the head usher takes the best man's and groom's boutonnière to the vestry. The best man pays 'the officiant' either before or after the ceremony.

The procession may include ring-bearers for both rings – traditionally a 4–5 year old boy, often one little girl or two small girls carrying a velvet or satin cushion edge with lace with the groom's ring for the bride on it, and two other children, boys or girls, carrying the ring from the bride to the groom.

The Best Man's Wedding Reception Speech

At the wedding reception the best man gives the first toast to the bride or groom as soon as the champagne is poured. A longer speech is optional and often has a fairly impromptu air, although he may have made notes and privately gone over what he wanted to say beforehand. A summary or expansion of what he and others said at the bachelor party will be news to the rest of the audience. The speech features the bride and groom. He might talk about how he met the groom, how the groom has changed, what they have done together and why they are good friends.

Then he will mention the bride, explaining that when he first saw her he was so impressed that he wondered 'what does such a lovely girl see in you, my brother?', which is supposed to make the bride look better by comparison. Finally he might wish 'my brother and his lovely wife luck, love and happiness,' or 'peace and harmony,' or 'everlasting love and happiness'.

Homosexual Marriages

Homosexual marriages are conducted in communities such as San Francisco, usually by ministers who are themselves homosexual. Is there a best man or 'third man', a fourth man, or a groom's maid? Since the homosexual marriage is a recent innovation there is no tradition which you are obliged to follow. Certainly ushers can follow the practice of directing families and friends of each partner to the appropriate side of the church to join those they already know.

ISRAELI

A British boy marrying in Israel would have a best man although Israelis have no best men or ushers. The bridal car, carriage, or tractor, is decorated with flowers.

Weddings are often held outdoors with a canopy held aloft over the bridal couple. Check whether the canopy will be fixed in the ground on poles or held up. If it is to be hand-held, your four canopy holders should be lads of similar strength and height, and should practise co-ordinating.

Check the appropriate clothing. Men in the immediate family wear suits and ties. On an Israeli kibbutz in the hot summer the guests might arrive wearing shorts. Extra food is prepared because food is inexpensive and catering is not elaborate, so uninvited friends of guests are welcome.

MIDDLE EASTERN AND ARABIC

In Tunisia you may be in a wedding reception hall with men only, while the bride sits in state on a throne with the women in another hall.

As always make yourself agreeable by finding out whether there is anything you can do to help and expressing an interest in the family, but find out about local etiquette. In some countries you should enquire after the health of a man's family. Do not pay direct compliments to or about his wife, as this will offend him or at least make him distinctly nervous. That is like saying to an Englishman, 'I've noticed that your wife is extremely attractive, and has lots of sex appeal. She's very interesting. In fact, I rather fancy your wife.'

A way round this, if you do not know the bride well, is to ask the bride's fiancé or father, 'Tell me about yourself and the bride and her/your family', or 'Tell me more about your daughter/your new wife and where she has been/will be living.' When you learn of her talents and achievements you can say to the bride's father, 'You must be very proud of her and her good work,' or 'She is a credit to you'; to the groom's parents, 'She will be a credit to your family'; or to the groom, 'I am very pleased for you," or 'She will be a credit to you'.

In some communities you should not ask too closely about the future plans and hopes because this might bring bad luck (the evil eye), and because only God can decide the future. Remarks by your host and yourself may be prefaced by 'God willing ... we/you/they will ...'. When you have established the rules, you can brief other ushers or guests from your home as to correct behaviour. If they act inappropriately it may be better to explain their actions to your hosts, rather than making the guests unduly embarrassed after the event.

In some Middle Eastern and European countries you are expected to pin money onto the dress of the bride as a wedding present. Have a supply of paper money ready – crisp, clean new notes.

ORIENTAL & OTHERS

Japanese
The Japanese require guests to remove shoes when entering buildings. At private homes slippers for guests are kept just inside the door. This will apply to a Japanese home in London, just as much as a temple in Tokyo.

Indian
Although Indians are predominantly Hindu, and Pakistan is officially Muslim, members of other religions live

in both countries, and there are numerous religious groups, such as the Sikhs, as well as many languages.

Hindu

Remove shoes when entering a temple – a general practice in very hot countries. On entering a Hindu temple every person rings a bell to inform the God of their arrival. The Hindu groom traditionally tied a ribbon around the bride's neck and ties a knot in it – hence our saying tying the marriage knot. Parsees tie the groom's hands with a seven-stranded cord, seven being a sacred number.

ALCOHOL

Alcohol may be forbidden in India, as it is in Saudi Arabia, because the guests are Muslim, or Hindu. In addition there are laws concerning those who may be served drink, sometimes only foreigners in certain hotel bars which are granted licenses. The barman may be allowed to sell alcohol to foreigners who buy a club membership for a small fee, usually about the price of a drink. Other premises may not be allowed to serve alcohol, or there may be designated certain days when drink can and cannot be offered.

Certain towns in Scotland are 'dry' – forbid alcohol. The same applies to some counties in the USA – a leftover from the days of prohibition – and to church owned buildings in such areas as parts of Texas.

Humanist

Details of humanist weddings are available from the British Humanist Association.

REGISTER OFFICE

In a register office there is often not enough space for a large number of guests and so you generally do not need many, if any, ushers.

Clothing
As is the case with a church wedding, the bridal group should co-ordinate their clothing styles.

Speeches
The registrar will address the bride and groom and guests, welcoming them and explaining the procedure. They repeat after him a declaration that they are free to marry, call upon those present to witness the fact that they are marrying, and sign the register, followed by the witnesses. Then photographs may be taken of them pretending to sign the register.

Documents
You will require a certificate or certificate with licence.

Seating
Phone or visit the register office in advance. You will want to know which side of the building the car park and entrance are situated on, and whether the register office is up a flight of stairs or very near the main entrance.

The register office in a small town is often small, with about twenty seats. Out of town relatives who are staying with the family or at a hotel may wish to attend the register office, as they have come so far for the occasion. If there are insufficient seats, the best man and young ushers should stand in the side aisles and allow older relatives and bridesmaids to take the seats. The best man needs to be near the table to sign as a witness. The superintendent and registrar sign the register.

Transport
The register office may be a less identifiable landmark than a church and both local residents and out of town guests should have the address and/or map. For convenience of locating the building they may choose to drive in convoy to the register office at a sedate speed.

If you are all assembling at the bride's or groom's house to proceed together to the register office, arrange for the best man or an 'usher' to stand outside the house signalling to arriving cars that they have found the right place, and directing cars to parking spaces.

Timing is critical. You must not arrive more than fifteen minutes in advance or you will run into the previous wedding party, and you should not be late because there may be another wedding group arriving at the register office shortly after yours. Allow time to proceed to the register office in convoy. Apart from the dignity of a slow, unhurried progression, the leading car may need to wait for others who are delayed by traffic lights or at intersections.

Blessing

Some couples who are keen to be married in church but are unable to because one has previously been married will opt for a church blessing. If this takes place after the register office marriage and before the reception, you will have to take care of transport to and from the church venue in addition. The blessing ceremony may involve two ministers. Alternatively a couple who are of different religions might have two blessings in different churches – preferably not all on the same day!

On leaving the register office for the hotel or home where the reception is held, again a car driven by a local person can be appointed to lead the way.

The address of the hotel or other location will be on the invitation. But it is still useful to remind the drivers of the hotel name and best route before they drive off. Again a map may be helpful. With all this to-ing and fro-ing it would be worthwhile to do a re-run of the routes in advance on the same day of the week to check realistic timing. Take into account any foreseeable traffic delays, such as street markets or football matches, and if necessary plan a back route to avoid the centre of town.

After the wedding

When returning to the bride's home from the register

office, or back there after leaving the hotel reception for a small post-party party, check that out-of-town guests remember the house name or number. They may think that they will recognize it when they see it, but streets of almost identical houses seem to stretch on for miles late at night.

If you are staying with the bride or groom's family for a grand family reunion it is tempting to stay up late talking. Should you see signs that the bride's mother or father are getting tired, make a move to go to bed or offer to see other guests back to their hotels. Any elderly person, such as the bride's grandmother, or great-grandmother, may need to go home earlier than the late revellers.

Give your phone number to guests so that if anyone gets lost or has a problem and does not want to call the bride's house late at night, they can contact you.

Check the railway station to be sure that trains are on time, and tell departing guests that if they are delayed they should not spend all night on the station but call you.

Phone the airport to check that the bride and groom and other guests have caught the scheduled flights. If the bride and groom are delayed at the airport you can go out with some leftover champagne and canapes to keep them company. A Just Married sign and a camera would enable you to take a few photos to help pass the time for them. Alternatively, phone the airport or airline staff and see if you can get the honeymoon couple moved to a VIP lounge.

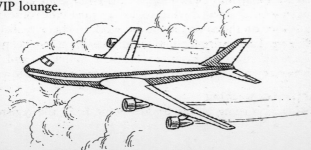

AFTER THE PARTY

After the party it seems as though everything is over, but for the wedding couple their life together is just beginning; and if you are the groom's best man you have proven yourself to be his most stalwart ally, and a reliable and trustworthy new friend for the bride. Your lifelong relationship with them as a married couple is just starting.

Back at the hotel where the reception is held you may be called to collect lost and found items. Technically the guests should depart after the bride and groom have left, and the hotel or hall may wish to lock up. But guests do not necessarily want to go back to their homes or work, leaving family and friends they have not seen for years. You must politely persuade happy guests to leave. If you wish, ask some of them back to your home (providing this does not rival a similar invitation to call at the bride's mother's home).

Transport

See that anyone inebriated is sent home safely in a taxi or under the care of a more sober driver. See the elderly or single safely to their homes by arranging lifts for them if they live at a distance, or take them back yourself if they live near your home.

Clothes

The morning after the party you will return your own and the groom's hired clothes to the hire company. Or you can take your clothes and his to the cleaners, later collecting them and returning the groom's clothes to his new home.

Gifts

If you have been safeguarding presents which were

delivered on the day to the reception hotel, or displayed there, you will take these to the groom's home immediately, or keep them at yours since it is safer in an inhabited house, and deliver them to the groom's home on the day he is due back.

The groom may ask the best man to order flowers, pot plants, a garden bush, or a fruit tree to be sent to the bride's mother with a thank you note from the groom the day after the wedding. This can be done through Interflora, and would be a nice gesture in winter or spring. However, there may be numerous flowers left over from the wedding, or the bride's mother might have an abundance of flowers in her own garden if it is summer time.

An alternative would be to send a large box of chocolates, a bowl of exotic fruit, a personalized gift, theatre, opera or ballet tickets, or a book or gift featuring the lady's favourite hobby or pastime. The best man might be able to suggest this to the groom, as well as making the necessary arrangements, and to find out what would please the bride's mother.

Personalized gifts are advertised in bridal magazines and Christmas catalogues, charity catalogues, mail order catalogues, and by mail order companies advertising in the popular tabloid newspapers as well as the heavy Sunday papers and their magazines, and general women's magazines. Libraries keep reference books listing major companies, department stores which deliver worldwide, brand names and products, plus specialist magazines advertising mail order goods. A handsome picture frame for the wedding photographs would certainly be useful.

Newspapers

You will need black and white photographs if you wish to send them to local newspapers. Newspapers can convert colour prints to black and white but this costs them time and money. If the local paper did not send a photographer you might like to despatch to the newspaper a wedding photograph and a typed note of who married whom, when, where, in what clothes, and where the honeymoon will be. Look at a previous issue of the paper to see how much detail they give. If you can mention the bride or groom's school or workplace, or where they will be working, that might increase your chances of getting them mentioned in the paper. If the bride or groom or either of their parents works in a local restaurant or large office or factory, that will be of interest to many of the newspaper's readers. Any minor disaster or narrowly averted calamity, (the car broke down on the way to church and the milkman gave the bride a lift!) should make the news page of the local paper, or one of the more popular nationals.

This information should reach the newspaper as fast as possible, while it is still news. You may wish to phone the newspaper to check their deadline and take the typed copy and photograph round to the newspaper in person.

Check when the vital edition of the paper will be appearing and buy at least one copy, preferably several. You might want to send clippings to relatives abroad, bridesmaids, ushers, and others, or have an extra copy to pin on the notice board where the bride and groom work.

Thank You Note
Finally you will thank the groom and bride in person and/or in writing for bestowing on you the honour of being their best man, or usher, for a delightful day, and for their thoughtful gift to you which you will treasure.

AFTER THE HONEYMOON

When the Bridal Couple Return

Naturally if you are the groom's best friend, immediately after the honeymoon either you will telephone him to ask how he enjoyed the destination and holiday, or he will phone you.

Unfinished New Home

If the builders and decorators have not kept to schedule the bridal couple might return from honeymoon to find their home not complete. The builder's excuse might be sickness, lack of staff, or the non-arrival of some vital part such as the cooker. The best man, if the bride and groom's parents are not nearby, could check that all is well while they are away, chase up the builders or supplier, and fix things up for the day of their return. He can turn on the heating, deliver flowers, fruit, milk, or food, and leave a note welcoming them back. He could also offer to invite them around for a snack or sandwich, or encourage the maid of honour to do so. Another possibility is to form the ushers into a painting party before or immediately after the couple's return to get at least one room ready.

No Photographs

Photographs can fail to arrive for a variety of reasons, such as the non-appearance of the photographer, the camera jamming, the flash failing, and batteries running out. Guests forget cameras, and run out of film. The pictures may be taken out of focus, with heads cut off, or the camera wasn't loaded.

Wedding photographs can be re-taken at a photographers studio, the bride's home or the hotel or other location, after the honeymoon. This is quite a common practice in America where the time-consuming posing of photographs by professional photographers would unduly delay the wedding reception.

Have a professional photographer in addition to your amateur photographers, but make sure you are not committed in advance to buying several expensive photographs. The photographer may charge such high prices that only a small number of framed photographs are ordered. Wedding guests may wish to pay the photographer for duplicates. But instead or in addition amateur snaps can be duplicated and given to the guests at less or no cost.

It is best to inform the local newspapers in advance so they can send their own photographer. Newspapers will sell photos to the public on request. Don't rely on the newspaper photographer's attendance. Any major event in the vicinity will deflect the photographer to news coverage. If the reception is in one district and the bride and groom live in adjoining areas, you may be able to inform more than one newspaper.

Duplicate copies of the local newspaper can be bought on the day of publication or later – usually for a slightly higher fee. With a bit of ingenuity the newspaper's front page masthead and the account of the wedding can be pasted together and photocopied to make a wedding poster, and reduced in size for sending airmail to relatives abroad.

The bride who is disappointed because she has no wedding day photograph will cheer up considerably if a posed wedding portrait is transferred to a souvenir wedding plate. Bridal magazines carry advertisements for such services. So do certain photographic suppliers, who duplicate photos and transfer them onto tablemats, greeting cards, and Christmas cards, particularly around Christmas time.

Post Honeymoon Film Show
Normally the bride and groom will be keen to entertain

in their new home and will first hold a get together to show their honeymoon slides, photos or videos. Naturally you will take round your photographs of the wedding and settle up any financial or practical arrangements, such as return of the deposit for the groom's hire clothes, or the receipt for the cleaning of the clothes for which he will reimburse you. You will be returning the telegrams and any other leftover items from the wedding. You may be required to load a projector or video screen for the slide film show.

WEDDING ANNIVERSARIES

You will want to send the bridal couple a card on their first wedding anniversary, when they may be holding a party to eat a tier of the cake they have saved. It is a good idea to contact the groom in advance and subtly remind him of the forthcoming date, and perhaps enquire what he will be getting his wife. If he has no idea you might tell him what the traditional anniversary symbol is. If the bride and groom hold a party each year these are the appropriate presents.

Wedding Anniversary Gifts

Traditional/Modern
- 1st Paper/clocks
- 2nd Cotton/china
- 3rd Leather/crystal/glass
- 4th Books/electrical appliances
- 5th Wood/silverware
- 6th Sugar, chocolates/wood The 'Wooden Wedding'
- 7th Wool, copper/desk sets
- 8th Bronze, pottery/linens, laces
- 9th Pottery, willow/leather
- 10th Tin, aluminium/diamond jewellery The 'Tin Wedding'
- 11th Steel/fashion jewellery
- 12th Silk, linen/pearls, coloured gemstones

13th   Lace/textiles and furs
14th   Ivory/gold jewellery
15th   Crystal/watches The 'Crystal Wedding'
20th   China/platinum The 'China Wedding'
25th   Silver The 'Silver Wedding'
30th   Pearl/diamond
35th   Coral/jade
40th   Ruby The 'Ruby Wedding'
45th   Sapphire
50th   Gold The 'Golden Wedding'
55th   Emerald
60th   Diamond The 'Diamond Wedding'
75th   Diamond

ONCE MORE?

The best man may have muddled through doing the minimum the first time around, or surprised and pleased both his family and friends by his efficiency. Either way, it is always easier to be best man the second time. If there is anything you would do better on a future occasion, make a note of it – or send a note to the publisher of this book so that we can incorporate your suggestions in future editions. Make a file labelled Weddings, if you have not done so already, and keep a copy of your speech, names of dress hire companies, music groups, the master of ceremonies, caterers and other supplies. While it is fresh in your mind, note whether you would avoid choosing them again, ask them to do things differently, or highly recommend them rather than any rivals who might be considered.

If you have shown yourself to be an efficient best man and an amusing speaker, perhaps you will be asked to be best man again. If the chief bridesmaid has caught your eye, or the bride's sister, or the happiness of the bridal couple has convinced you that it is time to settle down, perhaps you will get engaged and choose the groom to be your best man!

TROUBLESHOOTING GUIDE

Preventing and Dealing with Mishaps
Most mishaps at weddings are minor ones. Momentary embarrassments have included the missing ring, a missing organist, and microphones which don't work, difficulties which can soon be solved. I have also read news reports of weddings where the minister refused to marry the bride, or the wedding party guests were arrested for fighting! More serious difficulties at weddings of my family and friends have included missing wedding luggage (which appeared from the hotel luggage room at the end of the honeymoon), and wedding presents stolen from the boot of the car in the reception hotel car park.

The best way to prevent or put right these problems is to anticipate them and have contingency plans. Those who organize events regularly, whether caterers, or hotel managers, automatically arrange for a back-up plan to cover eventualities they have previously experienced, to guard against financial loss and guarantee goodwill. If you can learn from the mistakes of others you can avoid encountering major difficulties yourself, and you will have the confidence to face small hassles calmly and deal with them quickly.

THE WEDDING CEREMONY

Late Bride
Brides are often a little late. Exceptional lateness can be caused because the bride's car will not start, because town-centre traffic or a road accident is blocking the main road, or the hire car company has taken the bride to the wrong church.

A quick phone call to the bride's home around the time you expect her to leave, and/or after she should have left, will give you a clue as to what has happened. If she is arriving in an ordinary hire car, it should have a car phone so phone the head office and ask them to radio to the car to find out where the car and bride are.

You can fill in time by getting the organist to play more music, and send the ushers around talking to the guests and explaining what is happening before they get agitated.

Ceremony Etiquette

The minister and church authorities may object to the throwing of confetti (creating litter) the making of a video in church, or the recording of the choir, who may ask for additional fees. Check these points in advance. It may be possible to throw rice (an Indian custom) or flower petals rather than confetti, or to take the video of the couple entering church and the procession after the end of the ceremony itself.

Replacing a Lost Ring

Check that the ring is the right size for the bride. If she has put on weight the ring may be too tight. Her fingers may swell in summer time. See that the ring is insured. Store it in a safe place. Move it into a secure pocket immediately before the ceremony. Some jewellers will provide a spare ring of nominal value just in case. In theory if the ring is forgotten or lost inside the coat during the ceremony – or rolls off down the aisle, time can be saved by passing the bride another ring.

However, the ring is supposed to be a token of the groom's offer to support the bride financially, and a Jewish marriage may be invalid if the ring does not belong to the groom or his family, or the bride is misled as to the value of the ring. The best solution is for a spare ring to be worn by the groom's mother, which can be swapped over later.

An Invalid Ceremony

If the wording is incorrect, or the best man ends up

married to the bride, the ceremony can be repeated immediately. If it is discovered at a later date that the ceremony was invalid, if the minister was bogus, for example, it can be repeated at the time of discovery.

Spilt Wine

The worst problem is red wine – on a white dress. You might ignore this and leave the problem to the maid of honour – unless it's your glass of wine which got spilt over the bride's dress. Perhaps champagne or sparkling white wine is chosen for weddings for good reason.

The Jewish groom and bride however sip a cup of red wine during the wedding ceremony. This is supposed to add joy to the occasion, not to be a test of steady hands and good housekeeping.

If the groom or bride spill wine, first she should wash the stained area immediately. If the bride has a dress made to order she can carry a handkerchief of the same material, and in the event of a mishap this can be pinned or sewn over the stain to look like a pocket.

If the accident happens late in the day the bride can change into her going away outfit early. A professional photographer will have taken photographs all day, starting with the bride in her dress at home with her parents before she leaves for the wedding ceremony, so there should be some photographs of her in the immaculate dress.

No Organist

It would be useful to have the home phone number of the organist and any stand-in who can take over if the organist falls sick. If your guests include musicians there may be one who plays the church organ and can take over.

Change of Minister

Sickness in the family – anything from bridesmaids with chickenpox, to the death of a parishioner requiring the minister's attendance at a funeral, can mean that the date chosen for the wedding is no longer possible for the preferred minister. It is a good idea for the best man, groom and bride to meet other ministers to the same congregation so that they feel at ease if there is a last minute change.

Toddler Horrors

Babies and toddlers can cry through the ceremony, crawl the wrong way up the aisle, laugh or wet themselves, fight over the ring, injure themselves on rose thorns, eat the icing off the wedding cake, or merely turn up when uninvited. But the bride loves the little darlings, doesn't she? So the bride's sister, the little darlings' mother, will tell you.

During the wedding ceremony ushers should seat guests with babies and young children in aisle seats for a quick exit and as near the back as possible. Alternatively a children's corner can be created with a nanny or childminder while the parents are engrossed in the ceremony. (You'll need to check with the officiating minister if this is possible.) Ushers and other uncles and close friends should have child-distracting toys or games ready. At the first whimper the child can be removed. If the parent asks why you can explain that you thought little darling was crying because he wanted to go to the toilet.

At a hotel wedding reception the tinies can enjoy a separate room with special treats for them. Ushers at the exit door of the kiddie room and the entrance door to the main hall can fetch parents to the kiddie room if the children want their parents.

If the wedding reception is held at home the children can be placed in a separate room with children's size tables and chairs, suitable foods, and entertainment. The bride should visit them at some point so they can see her, and be photographed with her, preferably before they are covered with sticky cake.

No Car

If the groom's hire car fails to turn up in time, or his own car refuses to start or runs out of petrol, the best man must be prepared to provide transport quickly by paying for a taxi or using his own car, which of course is in perfect running order and filled up with petrol. If the best man's car is not nearby he calls upon his mother, father, the groom's father or brother, his own or the groom's boss or employee, landlord, a passing police car, or whatever his initiative suggests.

Parking Ticket

Everybody loves a lover and most people love weddings. You can get away with anything if you're in the process of getting married. One bridal attendant received a parking ticket while the wedding ceremony was in process, but when he explained the circumstances to the police they tore up his parking ticket!

THE WEDDING RECEPTION

Shortage of Drink

If you run out of drink, go home and raid your drinks cupboard, or get front doorkeys and go to the bride's father's house for extra drink. Drive to the nearest off-licence and get more drink and glasses. At a sit-down dinner, caterers usually allow a certain number of bottles per table. Some hotels providing catering will not permit you to take in your own drinks. Others are flexible. If just a small number of elderly guests want port or after-dinner liqueurs which were not in the original budget, you may need to obtain some.

Leftover Drink

The groom or bride's father or whoever is paying for the wedding should have discussed what will happen to opened or unopened bottles of drink. Are these provided on sale or return basis, perks for the caterer's staff, or paid for whether used or not by the host and therefore his property to take away? If the latter is the case the leftover bubbly can be collected and given to the newly weds in their honeymoon suite, sent to their new home or delivered to the father-in-law who has paid for the wedding.

Similar questions can be raised concerning the flowers. Can the cost of church flowers be divided between the two or more wedding groups using the same church? Can the cost of table decorations be divided between two wedding parties using the same hotel restaurant on the same day? If not, are the flowers merely hired, or are they the property of whoever pays for the wedding?

If flowers belong to a groom who is paying for his second marriage, he may wish to have leftover flower displays sent up to his honeymoon suite, given to his mother, mother-in-law and bridesmaids, distributed among the guests, or saved for planting in his garden or placed on the windowsill of his new home. If the groom is flying off, the best man might assist the bride's mother, with the help of the ushers, in distributing the flowers.

Shortage of Staff

At one wedding I attended the caterers placed the food buffet style although a sit down dinner had been ordered. The caterer said there were not sufficient staff to serve all the food at the tables, and staff had been paid to serve a buffet, but not wait at table. As many guests had travelled distances, and elderly relatives were expecting a sit-down dinner, this was not acceptable. The bridal group considered asking the hotel management to supply extra staff. They could also have had the ushers deliver platters to every table, but this would have meant they had to leave the top table and female guests alone at the young people's table.

The solution reached was that the ushers placed *hors d'oeuvres* platters on the dinner tables. The bride's father tipped the serving staff extra to wait at table providing the main course and dessert. The financial dispute with the caterer was sorted out later.

Missing or Marred Clothes

Cuff-links can be replaced with others, and big buttons replaced by smaller buttons – the chances are most people will not notice. If major items go missing the possible remedies are to go home and look again, buy, borrow, or improvise. Large hotels sometimes keep spare ties and bow ties for restaurant guests.

If the reception is being held at a grand hotel where the honeymoon couple will be staying for the first night of their honeymoon, your guests probably include VIPs already well known to the staff. But it is always worthwhile getting to know the head receptionist, hotel duty manager, restaurant manager or head chef. Then if a problem occurs later you will feel at ease phoning your contact on the hotel's internal phone or going round to see them.

You will be surprised at the staff's helpfulness and ingenuity in solving problems. A missing buttonhole can be replaced by one from the hotel garden, or a flower arrangement replaced by a girl who has much more skill with a piece of wire and tin foil than you would have. A professional chef can rescue the sinking wedding cake in a trice. A trainee waiter will be delighted to demonstrate napkin folding and make hats for small children.

Lost Rings – Again!

The best man is not the only one who might lose a ring, but he can be trusted to help if a ring is lost. The best man might suggest engraving the rings with the owner's name, and he may be able to track down missing rings – about which the public seems singularly sympathetic.

Engraving his and hers wedding rings with the names of the bride and groom and dates of the marriage is not a one hundred per cent guarantee that a determined thief will be discouraged from keeping or disposing of rings. But it does help a public-spirited finder to trace the grateful loser.

The groom's receipt for the ring, the valuation for insurance, and a photograph of the ring on the bride's hand, will be useful in advertising a reward, issuing notice of the loss to the police, claiming insurance for a loss, or obtaining an identical replacement.

I lost my ring which I had left in the hotel bedroom and hesitated to ask the chamber maid in case she thought I was accusing her of stealing it. I told the best man who had no hesitation in asking the hotel if anyone knew where it was. The hotel staff showed me they had merely placed it for safekeeping in the top drawer of the bedside table. Top marks go to the hotel whose member of staff found a man's wedding ring left behind on the hotel bedroom washbasin, and rushed to return it to him at the local airport.

A Lost Speech

You should keep duplicate copies of your speech and the groom's in a place where the duplicates can be found in a hurry. A long speech is best retrieved. If the speech is short you will have to extemporize. The rehearsal of the speech the night before will alert you to the location, or absence of the vital notes, and the rehearsal will enable you to remember the gist of both speeches.

Drunk, Sick or Silent Groom

The drunk groom or guest can be sobered up with water, food, and coffee. Prevention is better than cure. If a drunk groom gets to the microphone you will have to get him away as fast as possible. Pretend the groom was joking. If necessary switch off the microphone or the amplifier and get the band to strike up. Improvise something such as, 'I don't know if you all caught that, the groom actually said, in Esperanto, that he wanted everyone to start dancing.'

The sick groom or guest can be removed to the cloakroom or taken to a bedroom to lie down. You can say he just went out for some fresh air and will be back shortly. If he looks seriously ill of course phone your home doctor, the ambulance service, or get the hotel to call a doctor. If you have a large number of guests you can appeal for a doctor or nurse. This may alarm the other guests. As soon as possible put their minds at rest by informing them that nobody is about to drop dead in their midst. Tell them if the guest will rejoin them shortly, has gone home, or been taken to hospital. If he regularly has such turns and recovers from them they will be glad to know that too.

If the groom is totally silent when he should give a speech you will have to say something funny to cover up. For example, 'He promised he would not give a long speech, and he didn't. Would you like to hear it again? It was better the second time, wasn't it?' or, 'He's shy and hates making speeches so as I am the best man I am going to thank (name) and propose the toast,' or 'He's the strong silent type, but he just muttered to me that if he's employing me as best man, I should do the work of speechmaking!'

Stopping Arguments and Preventing Fights

Saying 'Come outside' has many advantages. By the time you get outside the argument may not seem so serious. Insults repeated in front of a lamp-post are not so annoying as those said in front of your family and friends. The dangers of wrecking the hotel property, the decorations, or picking up wine and food and throwing are reduced. The cause of the dispute may have been left behind. Other guests are not drawn into a fight which can become a free for all. You can offer some threat, bribe, or apology you might not make in front of others.

Missing Persons

Keep a check on the whereabouts of the bridal group,

and notice if any of the chairs at the wedding dinner remain unoccupied in case a guest has got lost. If the bride's mother's house has an answering machine, check back for incoming messages from anybody who has got lost – they may say they have given up and gone back to their hotel, in which case you can contact them.

Outgoing messages should not reveal that the family is away but say that you are very busy and if the caller wants to check wedding arrangements call the number of the hotel where the reception is held. That will give anybody who is calling to say they are lost a number from which they can obtain directions to the hall.

Entertainers

Entertainers should be selected by going to hear them play, and instructing them as to the volume of sound and variety of music required. You need to make it clear how long they are required to play, to find out what will happen regarding substitution if any of the band fall ill. They might break down on the motorway or lose their way. Their equipment could develop faults. If you have a back-up system, such as cassette playing equipment, friends who have guitars nearby, or if the hotel where the reception is held can supply music tapes and players at short notice, you are well prepared.

Missing or Stolen Wedding Presents

You will need to list all the presents and their values in order to inform the police and the insurance company. Stolen cheques can be cancelled. Notify the senders and banks immediately. The bride and groom will cheer up if replacement gifts can be ordered from the stores.

Finding Lost Travel Tickets

If both the groom and best man think the other has the travel tickets you must reconstruct where you last saw them, the location, and the clothes you were wearing, and where you have been since. Tickets for scheduled flights can be replaced more easily than those for package tours. Given lack of time you will have to try to queue-jump and see supervisors rather than wait in long lines only to be referred elsewhere. Any other documents you may have – such as hotel numbers, phone numbers of travel agents and so on, will be useful.

THE HONEYMOON

Honeymooners like to escape from the cares of home and work and keep their destination a secret from family and colleagues who might phone up and disturb them. Brothers who might play practical jokes are not given hotel phone numbers and addresses. However, if the groom trusts the best man he would give him a number to be contacted in emergencies – such as the illness of a parent at home. Nowadays most ferries, trains, and planes have telephones.

The time when it is hardest to contact a couple is when they are motoring, with hotel destinations picked on a daily basis. One way to contact them as they travel is to put out an appeal over a radio station. If the couple do not hear it on the car radio, they may be identified by hotel staff or hotel guests when they stop.

Another way of contacting the honeymoon couple who are travelling across several countries through Europe or elsewhere is to contact an embassy abroad. They will notify the border crossing officials who will ask the couple to contact the embassy for information.

Honeymoon Beds

Hotels with several ballrooms can hold up to five weddings the same day on a busy Saturday in springtime or summer. The wedding couples may be given a free bedroom in which to change clothes, or a free bedroom in which to stay the night before flying off the next day. The honeymoon couple are sometimes told that they will receive the honeymoon suite with the four-poster bed and/or Jacuzzi or the best available room. If there is only one honeymoon suite with a four-poster bed it can only be given to one of the honeymoon couples, or it may be given to a paying guest, not to any of the honeymoon couples.

Passports
The usual system is for a bride to apply several weeks in advance for a new passport in her married name to be issued dated from the day of the wedding. The bride can travel with a passport which is still in her maiden name. Many married women continue to use their maiden names.

When the bride, groom, best man or usher urgently needs a new passport because of losing the passport in a burglary or needing to travel unexpectedly because of sudden illness in the family abroad, you will need to provide documentary evidence such as a police report, doctor's letter on headed notepaper, or telegram.

Sometimes passports are left behind when travelling on the honeymoon and again package tour operators may help the honeymoon couple to re-route – to see Niagara Falls from the American rather than the Canadian side for example, or the Canadian side if a US visa has not been obtained. Crossing borders is much easier if you have good evidence of your identity. Passport photos are useful for obtaining identity cards. Advise the groom to take with him identity cards which contain his photograph and signature, a professional membership card, or a driver's licence to show his age and address.

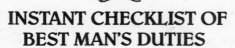

INSTANT CHECKLIST OF
BEST MAN'S DUTIES

Although not all of these duties may apply to the
wedding you are attending, it is useful to check that these
eventualities have all been considered.

BEFORE THE WEDDING

- Meet bride, and parents of bride and groom
- Appoint ushers or discuss their appointment with
groom
- Attend engagement party
- Organize or attend stag party
- Organize or discuss seating at church, register office
and reception with bride's mother
- Check through necessary documents with groom:
reading of banns, marriage licence, marriage
certificate
- Check through necessary clerical payments with
groom: minister, choir, bell ringers, organist
- Arrange transport to church for self and groom, and
check transport arrangements for bride, and to
reception
- Arrange hire of clothes for self and groom
- Organize buttonholes for self and groom, and ushers
- Discuss music, bells, flowers with groom, bride and
bride's mother

WEDDING MORNING

- Collect hired clothes for self and groom if not before
- Dress, and check groom's outfit
- Collect buttonholes
- Liaise with bride's mother over any last minute chores
- Take wedding ring and any honeymoon documents
from groom for safekeeping
- Entertain groom until ceremony

AT THE CEREMONY

- Conduct the groom to the church or register office in good time and take up position
- Produce ring when required
- Sign register
- Join procession out of church
- Take part in photographs and help find needed relatives or bridesmaids
- Help with transport from the ceremony to the reception

AT THE RECEPTION

- Supervise ushers and parking arrangements
- Receive and introduce guests
- Make speech on behalf of the bridesmaids
- Hand over honeymoon tickets, car keys etc. to groom before departure
- Organize decoration of car
- Supervise loading of luggage

AFTERWARDS

- Assist bride's mother in clearing up after the reception
- Return hired clothes of self and groom
- Take wedding presents to the couple's new home
- Check arrangements for couple returning from honeymoon and arrange to meet them or a welcoming gift

INDEX

American weddings, 62, 65–8

bachelor parties 29, 65
best girl 12, 19–20, 29
best man
  accepting role 14–15
  arrival at church 42
  choosing 8–13, 15, 19
  duties 30–6, 33, 37, 71
  expenses 10–11
  wife or girlfriend of 16–17
bride
  late arrival 81–2
  pre-wedding meeting 30
buttonholes 16, 40–1, 67, 87

cake cutting 52–3
children
  at church and reception
    18, 40, 52, 84
  of first marriage 15
church blessing 72
Church of England
  weddings 60–1
clothing 51, 65–6, 70
  best man or girl 15–16,
    19–20
  buttonhole or corsage 16,
    19, 20, 38, 40–1, 67, 87
  groom's 36
  guests' 39
  hired 15, 30–1, 34, 35, 57,
    58, 74
  informal weddings 58
  matching ties etc. 16, 66
  missing or marred 87
confetti 82

dancing at reception 55–6
divorced
  bride or groom 62

parents 39–40
double wedding 45
dress see clothing

entertainment
  choosing 90
  stag party 23–7
expenses 33, 44, 64, 82
  best man and ushers
    10–11
  stag party 21

fees for clergy etc, 44, 60, 82
flowers 16, 19, 20, 38, 40–1,
  67, 87
French weddings 65

gifts
  missing or stolen 90
  to bride's mother 75
  wedding 16, 17, 30, 33,
    74–5
Greek Orthodox weddings
  65
guard of honour 45

hen party 28, 29
Hindu weddings 70
hired
  car 24, 31–2, 34, 82
  clothes 15, 31, 34, 35, 57,
    58, 74
homosexual marriages 67–8
honeymoon 33–4, 56–7, 73,
  91–2
Humanist weddings 70

Indian weddings 69–70
informal weddings 58–9
insurance 34, 88
invitations
  stag party 21

wedding 17
Israeli weddings 68

Japanese weddings 69
Jewish weddings 60, 62–4,
  83

marriage licence 33, 37, 71
Middle Eastern and Arabic
  weddings 68–9
Muslim weddings 64

newspapers, photographs
  for 75–6, 78
non-conformist weddings 62

passports 34, 42
photographs 45, 56, 58, 78
  at stag and hen parties 24

reception arrangements
  51–7, 59, 67, 72–3, 85–6
  staff shortages 86–7
  transport 46
recession 44–5
register, signing 6, 44
register office weddings 70–3
rings 9, 42–3, 64
  insuring 34, 88
  lost 82, 87–8
  ring bearers 67
Roman Catholic weddings
  61–2

seating arrangements 31, 36,
  39–40, 71
  reception 52
second marriages 15, 20, 62
signing the register 6, 44
speeches 53–4, 71
  best man's 9, 16, 35,
    47–50, 67
  lost notes 88
  stag party 27–8
stag party

arranged by best man
  21–9
  car hire 24
  date and location 21–3, 35
  entertainment 23–7
  paying for 21
  photographs 24
  refreshments 22–3, 25

telegrams 54–5
transport
  best man's duties 31–3,
    37–8, 74, 85
  car hire 24, 31–2, 34, 82
  informal weddings 58, 59
  parking arrangements
    37–8
  problems 85
  register office weddings
    71–2
  to reception 46
travel expenses, best man's
  10–11

umbrellas 38
ushers 45, 55, 56, 67
  arrival at church 37, 38
  behaviour 40–2
  choosing 11–12
  duties of 6, 31, 38–9, 46
  girlfriends 18
  pre-wedding meeting 30

vaccinations 34
video films 24, 79, 82

wedding
  anniversaries 79–80
  gifts 16, 17, 30, 33, 74–5
  invalid ceremony 82–3
  invitations 17
  rehearsal 36, 65
  rings 9, 34, 42–3, 67
wet or snowy weather 38
wine, spilt 83